'... calmness rare in my life, and over the weeks
felt more positive, less stressed and sharper somehow.
I was also left wondering why something so simple
isn't available on the NHS.' – *The Sunday Telegraph*

'Sophrology looks set to be the next buzzword
answer to all our problems.' – *The Guardian*

'Sophrology is big news in the wellness world.' – *Elle*

'Sophrology is set to be the next wellness trend . . . If it's
used effectively by everyone from women in labour to
Olympic athletes, it can only be a matter of time before
Sophrology enters our wellness lexicon.' – Refinery29

'While many people try and fail to reap the benefits of
meditative practices, taking up Sophrology could be the key
to unlocking your mind's potential.' – *The Independent*

'The science is there. Resilience, better sleep and less stress?
This is one wellness trend we'll be watching.' – Get The Gloss

'You've heard of mindfulness, now meet its dynamic
young cousin Sophrology.' – *The Observer*

'Though Sophrology has been popular in France and
Switzerland for decades, the trend has been slow to
hit the UK. But awareness is starting to grow, though,
thanks to author Dominique Antiglio's best-selling book,
The Life-Changing Power of Sophrology.' – *Glamour*

'The simplest, most natural way of calming and focusing our lives lies in front of our noses, breathing. This book will transform all our lives if we follow its helpful suggestions.'
– Sir Anthony Seldon, vice-chancellor at the University of Buckingham and Co-Founder of Action for Happiness

BIOGRAPHY

Photograph © Simon Way

Dominique Antiglio is a highly qualified and globally sought-after Sophrologist specialising in stress management, self-development and birth preparation. Born in Switzerland, Dominique started Sophrology at 15 years old to overcome health issues, learning early on ways to positively connect with herself and embrace a new way of living.

She gained her Masters in Caycedian Sophrology (2006) notably with Professor Caycedo, the founder of the method in Spain. She is a graduate of the renowned European School of Osteopathy in Kent, UK, ran a successful osteopathic clinic for a decade in Switzerland, and holds a Holistic Voice Diploma (UK).

In 2011, having witnessed so many positive changes through the power of Sophrology for herself and her clients, she moved to London and founded BeSophro. BeSophro is now a leading Sophrology clinic with an online platform to support and inspire people in finding a calmer and happier life through the practice of Sophrology.

Her best-selling book, *The Life-Changing Power of Sophrology* is the first widely published book on Sophrology in English and is now a leading authority on the subject. It has been instrumental in spreading the practice beyond continental Europe.

Dominique's expertise is regularly sought in the media and her work has been featured in *The Times*, *The Guardian*, *ELLE* and *Marie-Claire*. She is also a regular workshop host, speaker and travels the world teaching people about the power of Sophrology to transform their lives. In 2015, Dominique became a mum.

To find out more about BeSophro classes, workshops, online programmes or to join Dominique's community, please visit www.be-sophro.com.

For my son Eliott,
For my husband Frédéric,
with joy, gratitude and infinite love.

THE LIFE-CHANGING
POWER OF SOPHROLOGY

....

Breathe and Connect with the
Calm and Happy You

DOMINIQUE ANTIGLIO

First published in Great Britain in 2018 by Yellow Kite
An imprint of Hodder & Stoughton
An Hachette UK company

First published in paperback in 2019

1

Copyright © Dominique Antiglio 2018
Illustrations © Juliet Percival 2018

The right of Dominique Antiglio to be identified as the Author of the Work has been asserted by her in accordance with the Copyright, Designs and Patents Act 1988.

A CIP catalogue record for this title is available from the British Library

Paperback ISBN 978 1 473 66265 0

Typeset in Warnock Pro by Hewer Text UK Ltd, Edinburgh
Printed and bound in Great Britain by Clays Ltd, Elcograf S.p.A.

Hodder & Stoughton policy is to use papers that are natural, renewable and recyclable products and made from wood grown in sustainable forests. The logging and manufacturing processes are expected to conform to the environmental regulations of the country of origin.

CONTENTS

INTRODUCTION

'My breath feels deep and calm as I tune into its comforting, rhythmic presence. Sitting in a simple desk chair, I am aware of my entire body relaxed. I am filled with lightness and a sense of a delicate flow of energy through my body. I am alive and present. My body feels warm and slightly heavy. With each breath, I feel a deep sense of confidence that further grounds me as excitement spreads through my body and mind. I intuitively know that all is possible and that no matter what happens, everything will go well . . .'

This is how I felt during my Sophrology practice on the day for which I had waited and prepared for so long. I was leaving Switzerland, my home country, for London! I had handed over the keys of my flat and the car was packed. I felt so ready for this new adventure. Yes, there were a lot of unknowns; I had sold my thriving practice as an osteopath and wouldn't be near my native 'tribe' – my family and friends – any more. I had decided to embrace the next steps of my life, which I knew would be with Sophrology and living in the city I loved most. I had been given so much over the many years I had studied and practised Sophrology, a treasure I was now ready to share. I was ready for a new challenge.

Getting to that moment was a long story. Sophrology had taught me how to stay calm and focused even in challenging and uncertain times, and therefore I felt well equipped for what was to come. It felt very freeing to be able to listen to the deep call of my true self and be authentic and positive about my life choices.

If you are reading this book, you are probably looking for or already in your own process of change. It is often hard to know where to start when we are faced with difficulties or when we desperately need to bring more calm and focus into our lives. As a Sophrologist, I am concerned at how our modern society and communities force us towards an overwhelming everyday life. Juggling roles and tasks at home, feeling defined by our financial worth and what we do, and managing the constant bombardment of communication from our 24-hour workplaces and social media is pushing people beyond their physiological limits. And it has become the new norm. Even with the best intentions, this can leave us feeling chronically stressed; suffering from anxiety; lacking confidence or clarity; or struggling with health, work or relationship issues. It's difficult to find the space to bring balance to our lives and listen to our true self if we are so busy just surviving. But we don't have to endure stress, pain and tiredness – there is a way to gain awareness of and transform the way we feel, and to truly thrive.

Widely followed in Europe, Sophrology was created 60 years ago in Spain by Professor Alfonso Caycedo. He was a psychiatrist and neurologist searching for a gentle practice to ease the physical and mental stresses of daily life for his patients, and develop harmony of body and mind. Decades ahead of the recent popularity of mindfulness, Sophrology – or 'dynamic relaxation' – has been shown to be an effective tool in dealing with stress and associated issues, allowing us to nurture and develop our inner resilience, confidence and clarity. It opens our minds to new perspectives and helps us face life challenges in a positive way. Its unique blend of Eastern philosophy and practices with Western science makes it a highly contemporary way to tap into our own inner 'superpowers' – using simple tools that draw on relaxation, meditation, breathing, visualisation and body awareness exercises.

Now, with this first comprehensive Sophrology guide in the English language, you can start to change your life – today. The joy of Sophrology is that everything you would like to reach is already within you. And the great news is that finding balance and calm doesn't require twenty years of studying ancient manuscripts or living only on avocado juice. Nor do you need to sign over the next three months of your life. In the midst of life's chaos, what if with just closing your eyes for just a few minutes a day and following some simple guided exercises, you could connect with this sense of balance and open a world of new possibilities in your everyday life?

Calm and happiness mean something different to everyone, and Sophrology will give you the tools to find it, by yourself and for yourself. As a woman, mother, wife, daughter and Sophrologist, the values of unity, sharing and gratitude are in my heart as I write this book. I strongly believe that Sophrology needs to be part of people's lives to support them on their path, in the same way as it has helped me so much. Just take a deep breath and dive into the world of Sophrology – this book may change your life . . .

PART 1

What is Sophrology?

My Story

'The real voyage of discovery consists not in seeking new landscapes, but in having new eyes.' *

MARCEL PROUST, *IN SEARCH OF LOST TIME*

'I didn't feel right.'

My journey with Sophrology began when I was 15 years old. I grew up in Fribourg, a small town in west Switzerland. I was a busy teenager, dividing my time between my academic work and playing basketball competitively. School was intense – like for many youngsters these days – and I didn't particularly enjoy it, being far happier on the basketball ground. I had a few close friends but wasn't very comfortable amongst people of my age. I was dreaming of the day I would be finished with school and the pressures that came with it.

* *'Le véritable voyage de découverte ne consiste pas à chercher de nouveaux paysages, mais à avoir de nouveaux yeux.'*

3

I had been suffering for a while – I was aware that I didn't feel good, I didn't feel right. I was constantly tired, and often lightheaded and struggling with dizziness, to the point that I even fainted a few times. My energy levels weren't good and doing my daily activities had become a real challenge. It felt like I needed so much sleep just to be able to function. I had a few infections and took a long time to recover from them, and never felt really 'well'. My parents had taken me to the doctor but they said they didn't know what was going wrong with me and I was quite worried.

We decided to talk to a lovely doctor, Maurice, an experienced and wise GP who was also a family friend. He arranged some blood tests and suggested medication as my blood pressure was always very low. The blood tests didn't show anything wrong and the medication didn't change anything, so after a few weeks it was increased, but still nothing improved, so it was increased again, but still no improvement. Maurice told me, 'There's nothing physically wrong with you.' He didn't know what was making me so weak. Not knowing and not understanding why I felt this way constantly was very worrying for me – it was as if my body was letting me down.

So Maurice suggested we tried something 'different' and look beyond medicine. 'Soph-what?' was my response when he told me about Sophrology. It was the first time someone had mentioned Sophrology to me or to my parents, but I decided to give it a try. At the time Sophrology was growing in popularity in Switzerland and offered to senior students to help them prepare for exams, alleviating stress and boosting confidence, as well as in high-level sport competition circles, as an aid to focus and improve performance.

'The next hour was going to deeply change my life.'

A week later, I found myself outside the door of Sophrologist Gill Thévoz, at her small Sophrology practice on the other side of town. My mum dropped me off and waited in the car. I remember standing at the door and wondering what was going to happen. I had no idea whether I was going to go through any tests or what Sophrology might involve, nor that the next hour was going to deeply change my life. It all felt very mysterious. When Gill opened the door I immediately felt welcomed. There was a warm and informal atmosphere with coloured cushions and comfy seats – it was very relaxed. She wasn't particularly tall but her presence was strong and her eyes very gentle. We had a little chat about my daily life and how I was feeling. Nothing too detailed – but it started a conversation. I was made to understand very early on that there were no rules, no requirements as to what I should think or feel in that room, that I could just be who I was. This felt new to me. It was a powerful revelation to me at a time when I was naturally absorbing pressures from my family, my teachers and my friends and peers as to what I should be doing and feeling. She seemed to find it OK that I didn't like school, and normal that I found myself feeling out of place in my environment: the fact that it all seemed to make sense to her was very comforting. She explained to me that the body and the mind are connected and that my dizziness and fainting episodes were perhaps related to how I was feeling deep inside. She offered to show me a few exercises to help me.

With my eyes closed, and guided by the most relaxing and gentle voice, Gill took me through a simple sitting relaxation exercise, then invited me to experience some standing work, using my breath and a few easy body moves. Everything felt effortless and uncomplicated. I remember mainly that it seemed very relaxing. For the first time, I was connecting to my breath and noticing its variation – and standing in a relaxed state felt very new. She asked me to listen for any sensation and I remember feeling light tingling down my arms and legs. The practices that we had worked through were recorded onto a tape (it was 1990!) and I was told to take away the tape and practise for about 10 minutes each day until the following week. And that was it.

'I immediately felt more positive and energised.'

I noticed a change in the way I was thinking after just that first session. My body also felt different. I had a sense of 'Things are not actually that bad, I think I can cope,' about my life, and I immediately felt more positive and energised. I didn't realise at the time but I was suffering from a lot of emotional stress, and it was clearly manifesting itself in my body as constant tiredness and difficulties coping with the demands of my teenage life. For the first time, I felt truly heard and understood. And the fact that I had been given something practical to do to feel better gave me hope again. I was being given the opportunity to connect with myself in a new way.

Every lunchtime – I came home from school to have lunch – I would switch on my tape recorder and practise in my room for 10 minutes. It was so helpful to have that time to connect – I didn't feel any pressure to do the exercises, it just felt like a good thing to do. I was slowly learning to listen to the sensations in my body, to control my breath and to focus my mind. I enjoyed that very much.

I had signed up for five appointments and after those first sessions I never, ever felt dizzy or faint again. After the five weeks, not only were my energy levels completely changed, but I also started to understand myself far more and appreciate the stress I was under. The recurrent infections cleared, my sleep was deeper, my body felt more relaxed and I had greater energy and positivity to study and train. It was as if I had gained a new perspective and confidence. Yes, I still had to do my homework, attend school and prepare for exams, but it all felt much lighter to experience.

'It was like being given a new life skill . . . my secret superpower.'

What was so immediately powerful for me was to be given special 'tools' – simple practices – to support myself. As

Gill explained to me, the exercises were helping me to relax and tune into a new place inside me, a place she called consciousness where all my potentials were hidden. The changes I felt after just these five sessions motivated me to go back and further explore what I could learn from this practice.

During my Sophrology sessions, whatever worry or difficulty I brought into the session, whether it was about my maths teacher or school exams (which I dreaded!), my family or friend relationships, my future or my health, there always seemed to be a way forward with it using the practice. Sometimes there was a solution, but more often I was just able to acknowledge the problem and see it differently, and that changed it into something I could live with more easily. Through Sophrology I became a receptor of something I felt was very special; it was like being given a new life skill, a way into my secret superpower 'consciousness'. I could be in the driving seat of my life rather than being the victim of challenges at school, or pressures at competitions, or tension with my family.

Using my breath to help let go of a worry or to connect with a state of confidence, consciously stopping to give time to my body and mind to recharge, and using Sophrology 'tools' to study more efficiently or feel positive about exams simply made my life more enjoyable again.

This is hugely valuable, especially when you are 15, as I started embracing my whole life with more meaning and learnt how to feel more in tune with myself. I think it protected me from a lot of potential problems and traps you can fall into around this age. It boosted my sense of self-esteem hugely, started to teach me about self-acceptance and helped me build my identity. It was such a big discovery that mind and body are connected, as was the realisation that my body had expressed discomfort as a reaction to the way I was managing my daily life, my mind and my emotions. Sophrology taught me to really believe in what I felt, rather than what my brain was telling me to do, or what others were doing.

'It became an important and everyday part of my life.'

After that first life-changing experience with Sophrology at 15, it became an important and everyday part of my life. The shift I experienced over the next two years was huge. Instead of worrying about my future, I had gained real confidence that the future was full of possibilities and, when it was time to choose a career path, I knew that I wanted to do something working with people and health. I spent a few weeks over the summer interning in a hospital in Geneva, which was an eye opener in terms of the medical care system. I came away disheartened by the pressure on the doctors and the lack of time for meaningful communication between patients and carers in this kind of environment. I wanted a job that would give me a greater connection with people, and a greater freedom. As I was researching other health professions, I was given a book on osteopathy.

Osteopathy seemed to understand that the body is connected with everything else and that we have a 'special power within' – called vitality in osteopathy – that positively affects the mind and body. It made sense to me, to view the body and mind beyond the strict science of medicine, and using my hands to support positive changes in people was very appealing. Osteopathy wasn't formally recognised in Switzerland at the time so I came to England to study for a degree in osteopathy.

'I wanted to learn what my Sophrologist knew.'

By the time I had finished my degree, I had also completed all 12 Levels of Sophrology with my teacher Gill. I returned to Fribourg to work as an osteopath and set up my own practice, and decided to train to become a Sophrologist as well. I wanted to learn what my Sophrologist knew – how Gill had been able to guide me all these years, using the infinite resource of Sophrology to help me be happier and healthier, make major life decisions and learn how to cope with the stresses of everyday life and my relationships. Finding my way through a happy life had been a challenge on many occasions – and every time we had been able to help me find the necessary inner resources to move forward.

As an osteopath, I looked at every patient through the lens of Sophrology as well, and the more I practised osteopathy with my clients the more I realised that their consciousness, emotions, way of thinking and their stresses impacted on their body's mobility and energy. The body never lies! At a very deep level I knew the power of Sophrology for myself, but as a practitioner to see that and to feel other people's bodies change as they practised Sophrology – I was reminded of the power of this tool.

I slowly increased my Sophrology practice, and then one day it was as if my hands had finished their work. That's how I felt, and I had to accept that my osteopathic life was at an end, and to surrender to a deeper call. And with that, I made the difficult and liberating decision to leave Switzerland and move to England – to embrace a new life as a fully practising Sophrologist.

'We have a choice in the way we live our lives.'

Fast-forward 10 years and my life now has very different challenges. I'm mum to a 20-month-old and run my own Sophrology practice in London. Whether I'm dealing with sleep issues or looking ahead to nursery and schooling for my child, preparing myself to guide a workshop or trying to find that holy grail of balance between work and home, life is even busier and more demanding. Thank goodness for Sophrology!

Its simple exercises still open up a world of possibilities for me. We all have stresses in our lives and we are given little help or training in how to deal with them. We are taught how to read and write but we don't learn how to be in ourselves, and accept ourselves. It is often only when we find ourselves in difficult situations or our health is compromised that we start listening. What is our body telling us? What does my headache, my difficulty sleeping or my anxiety tell me? Is there a correlation between this and what we feel deeply or aspire to? Nobody told me about the mind–body connection until I met Gill, and a lot of people haven't been given this knowledge. Ultimately, I think we all seek happiness and aspire to find balance in and enjoy our life, to be free from the things that block us or give us worry. We have a choice in the way we live our lives.

Sophrology doesn't have all the answers. I am still a work-in-progress, like everyone else living on this planet. Sophrology hasn't turned me into a superhero or a supermum who can manage everything, or who even wants to manage everything. I don't always have complete confidence and clarity. I think I perhaps just know better how to connect with my inner resources than before, and I am willing to listen and learn. Life is certainly much simpler, much healthier and happier than when I was 15, thanks to knowing myself better, having healed painful feelings and changed the outlook I have on my experiences.

Sophrology still helps me in my everyday life to feel more empowered, to live the life that I want and to find more meaning and joy. One of my greatest pleasures is to witness other people's success with it and how the uniqueness of every individual begins to shine more brightly through their daily life – when they reach that stage where they take responsibility for their situation and discover a way forward.

Why Do We Need Sophrology?

I talk often of the 'gentle superpower' of Sophrology, but its purpose is not to create 'superwomen' or 'supermen' of us but rather support individuals in knowing themselves, their strengths, their values and, very importantly, their limits.

When I guide my one-to-one and group Sophrology sessions, I see people from all different situations in life and with diverse experiences, backgrounds and emotions. They come to me with a huge variety of issues – from anxiety to sleep problems, lack of confidence or simply to prepare for an important event. What they all have in common is that they can no longer carry on in the way that they have been. They need something to change – for their happiness, for their health, for their career or for their reason to get up in the morning. Often for all of these.

I'm not a big fan of statistics, but I think we should all be talking about the research that tells us that stress, and particularly chronic stress, is a factor in five out of the six leading causes of death – heart disease, respiratory disease, strokes, cancer and fatal accidents. It is estimated that between 75 and 90 per cent of visits to the doctor are stress-related.

Having too much on is now seen as a good thing – juggling priorities, rampant social media and an endless list of things to achieve are viewed as a badge of honour. When do we ever stop and pause? When do we put ourselves first?

In our demanding world, filled with its overwhelming load, noise and stimulation, we have lost the connection between what we feel inside and what we see and experience outside. We have lost the ability to just be in the moment and listen to our deepest self.

Those who cope best with the stresses of modern life and find the greatest sense of happiness are the ones who can deal positively with these pressures, naturally or through personal self-help or some sort of discipline (such as sport, meditation or good nutrition). Perhaps they have a passion or hobby, a positive community around them (family, friends, partners) or strong values and a sense of purpose, knowing who they are. But, even with the best intentions and support, everybody can struggle at some point in their life and feel that something needs to change.

Sophrology offers the chance for you to pause, to connect with and clear stress today, and to channel your resources for a better tomorrow, true to your own self. It supports you to consciously and positively deal with difficulties and tensions, to find your place on this planet and create meaningful encounters with others.

'Talking to friends, I described it as: "I kind of felt like I was blocked and I wasn't connecting with myself, and I felt *that Sophrology basically gives you a safe environment with positive energy for you to release, learn how to focus and search internally for the answer that you need to really evaluate yourself in a non-judgemental way."* ' Beatrice

A Solution for Everyone

Many people I meet as a Sophrologist feel that they've already 'failed' at other forms of self-help because they couldn't 'do' them or didn't find the time or space in their life. I welcome them to Sophrology with the news that they are not required to do or be anything for the power of Sophrology to 'reset' their lives – they just need to start with giving themselves 10 minutes a day or 20 minutes three times a week to be guided in the practice.

Sophrology differs from other therapies in ways that make it so much more adaptable and easy to fit into our busy lives and to reflect who we are as people. There is no need to get changed or carry your yoga mat around – you can start your Sophrology practice in your office, at home or even as you commute. And you don't need to be able to stand on your head to be able to benefit from Sophrology, or even to stand or sit still for any length of time at all – it adapts for all physicalities and abilities.

Through my own interest in exploring what helps people to help themselves, what struck me straight away with Sophrology was that it required nothing from me, and that its powerful effects were immediate. As a teenager coming to Sophrology, I didn't have the time or inclination to spend hours learning new practices or ingesting information about how the body worked, and I didn't want to engage in something that meant I needed to talk about myself for hours. Already, I think I was looking for some way to be in control of myself – doing something to support my own body to look after itself rather than asking someone else to use their knowledge on me.

Through all my training and personal development I have become more and more aware that we are complex beings, and that our body, mind, soul, behaviours, beliefs, upbringing, relationships and lifestyle are all connected, and all influence us. On my quest to gain a holistic understanding of our complexity as a human being and on how to best engage in it as a therapist, I further trained and experimented with many approaches. My personal and professional journey has crossed the paths of acupuncture, homeopathy, Ayurveda, nutrition, reflexology, essential oils, yoga, Pilates, meditation, psychology, family constellation therapy, geobiology and sound therapy. I further trained in biogenealogy to understand how personal limiting beliefs and behaviours, often shaped by our upbringing and the life experience and dynamics of our family members and ancestors, can be understood and improved, or positively transformed. The simplicity of Sophrology, coupled with its deeply transforming power and adaptability, though, has always affected me most deeply. It doesn't ask us to believe in anything (it is more about learning to switch off our brain) or conform to any group, and it is a practice that encourages freedom, responsibility and non-judgement.

Body and Mind Together

While it shares many similarities with and benefits of mindfulness and meditation, Sophrology's power lies within the unique way it connects body and mind together to effect balance and change. You tap into the awareness of both to transform your state of consciousness and access your vital energy and most effective state of being. In a state of dynamic relaxation, you are shown how to use the simple breathing techniques, gentle movements and visualisations to allow you to explore your sensations, note your perception and develop your awareness, allowing its power to work on all areas of your life. Sophrology differs from many of the other therapies available in that:

- Its clear guided exercises allow you to start practising and feeling the effects straight away;
- It is adaptable to all styles of living, all levels of health and all schedules – you can complete the exercises at home or on public transport (or even hidden in the loo before an important meeting!);
- It's an easy way into meditation-type techniques. In a busy life, a lot of people find it hard to sit still and

meditate. Sophrology's simple step-by-step approach adapts to different needs and abilities so that everyone can access a meditative state and enjoy the many other benefits of this dynamic practice;

- Its practice will support you to overcome stress and help you find calm, positivity and greater awareness in your daily life. It teaches you to live more in the present moment, but it also helps you to transform your relationship with your future and your past;

- It doesn't ask you to unburden yourself of past issues, relationship problems or difficult histories – you can find your inner peace without analysis or deep examination;

- It complements other physical and psychological therapies, whether that be osteopathy, yoga or psychotherapy, and allows you to accelerate your progress and deepen your experience;

- There is no spiritual connection or association necessary for Sophrology – it is purely your own journey; you are not asked to work to any spiritual practice;

- And, finally, it teaches you a set of exercises and practices that you can use at any time and in any place to help you deal with what life throws at you. YOU become your own 'on the go' healer, with a personal supertool kit. And you regain the power to be in control of your own life.

The Big Difference Sophrology Makes

We live in a society that often looks for and values a quick fix for everything, and Sophrology definitely gives that. The Sophrology exercises are simple tools to use in your daily life, supertools to support you with a specific issue or to find the necessary focus to reach a goal. Whether you are looking for a new way to holistic health or to achieve a major objective in life, by using these tools, Sophrology can help you to:

- Learn to relax and let go;
- Overcome stress and decrease anxiety;
- Balance energy levels;
- Improve health and reinforce your immune system;
- Dramatically improve your sleep;
- Prevent burnout and physical/mental exhaustion;
- Develop self-awareness;
- Improve concentration, focus and memory;
- Increase confidence and self-esteem to allow you to achieve your goals;
- Help you perform to your best ability in challenging situations, such as presentations and speeches, exams, interviews, surgery, stage and sporting performances;
- Deal positively with anger and other emotions;
- Prepare for birth and parenthood;
- Be supported during illness and alongside medical treatment, notably for cancer, depression,

post-traumatic stress, postnatal depression, chronic fatigue and fibromyalgia;

- Learn to live in the present;
- Increase positivity and bring happiness in your daily life.

But it's more than just a short-term problem-fixer: through repetitive practice over time, Sophrology has the power to effect deep transformation in your life, allowing you to strengthen your inner resources and uncover your personal values. It encourages inner connection, positivity, to let go and trust, to be less judgemental of yourself and others. It helps transform your attitude towards yourself and your environment, making you more adaptable, creative and resilient. It may be used to deepen your self-development and boost your life skills, including:

- Improved resilience to daily life, difficult situations and relationships;
- The ability to plan for and make positive changes in your life;
- Increased creativity and intuition;
- Discovering and using your personal values to guide you in your daily life;
- Having a positive outlook on life: enjoying your present, being at peace with your past and motivated and confident about your future;
- Feeling at peace with yourself and the world around you.

It Starts with You

Most significantly of all, Sophrology comes from within ourselves. Sophrology is unique in the way it works directly with our personal superpower – our consciousness. Our consciousness is the energy within us, a vital power that organises and keeps our mind, body and soul in connection so we can function and live our existence. It's also what allows us to make choices in the way we respond to emotions, situations, people and events, and is the key to our inner resources of confidence, resilience, positivity and serenity.

What is Consciousness?

In Sophrology, we define consciousness as a power that animates us, an energy. This energy organises and integrates all the psychic and physical elements responsible for human existence. The state of our consciousness is directly linked to how we experience our life and how we perceive and interact with ourselves and the world around us. Through awareness, we can access this energy and support it in revealing its full potential to transform the way we live our life.

Sophrology gives us the tools to help us deal with our daily life and feel empowered to make our own choices. It means we can start to create the life we aspire to. The practice starts as you are guided into a slightly relaxed state of consciousness with your body fully relaxed and your mind focused. This is a state where you are more able to tune into consciousness and its potential, compared to when your eyes are open and you are engaging with the world around you. It is where we hold the power to connect with ourselves again, to relearn how to put aside the stresses and strains of the world around us.

What is Sophrology and Why Do We Need it? – Summary

- Sophrology is a dynamic relaxation practice to help you find happiness and balance in your life and give you the tools to cope with daily stresses and to help you reach your full potential.
- It is a guided practice combining breathing techniques, gentle movement, meditation and creative visualisation.
- Sophrology is quick, easy and adaptable. It excludes no one.
- Sophrology is an immediate solution to everyday issues like stress, lack of confidence and sleep problems, but practised over time it is able to transform your awareness and personal capacities for deep change.

CASE STUDY: **DANIEL** – '*I NOW UNDERSTAND THE POWER OF "STOPPING AND BEING".*'

Daniel came to me when he realised he was close to a crisis point in his life. He ran his own business, which at the time was under a lot of financial pressure. At home he had a young family, which he was finding stressful outside the workplace, and he was feeling pulled in many directions.

I thought I was just dealing with the normal stresses of trying to make big changes at work and being a good father, partner and son too. One day I felt I was having a panic attack when I missed an important presentation to a client. That was when I realised how bad things had got. I was very negative at work, short-tempered at home, couldn't sleep and was loaded with guilt about everything that didn't get done with my family. I'd completely lost myself. I wasn't doing anything well – I was going around in circles and making bad decisions because I was exhausted. And I wasn't able to think straight, or listen to myself.

When I started Sophrology, I wasn't sure about it. I'd always assumed that meditation and mindfulness wouldn't work for me, as I couldn't imagine finding the time or calm to be able to do them. I'm an active person – I want to do something to see results, not just talk about my life or sit and wait for something miraculous to happen in my head!

But I soon realised that it wasn't really about my head, and I didn't need to be able to breathe a certain way. I was doing small actions and thinking about what I needed and wanted, and trying to listen to my body. And I didn't feel I could do it at first. I wasn't feeling anything much in my body, but Dominique kept reminding me that I didn't need to 'be' anything or 'achieve' everything, so I just kept going. And I listened to the exercises on the train on the way to and from work – not great but the only time I had to myself.

Life felt different almost straight away. I had felt very lonely and powerless with all the pressures going around in my head all day long. But in Sophrology, we talked about the power of the mind–body connection and somehow my body seemed to share my pressure and I felt stronger, as if I could deal with things more. Life was easier. I learnt to use some of the 'tools' – The Shoulder Pump (page 113) when I was feeling stressed or 'in my head'. And The Bubble (page 135) to keep me clear of all the people and problems weighing me down in my daily life. I now understand the power of 'stopping and being', like Dominique tells me!

How Does Sophrology Work?

When Daniel first walked in to my Sophrology practice, he did not look well. He had a very stressful job and was struggling with the demands of life in general. I noticed immediately that his face was very red and his shoulders tense and raised. He struggled to sit down calmly – he couldn't stop fidgeting, twisting his hands together and I noticed him breathing fast with his chest. He wasn't at all keen to be in my office but was desperate. I knew that Sophrology could help him.

At the beginning of a session, people usually share why they have come, giving me an opportunity to understand their strengths and difficulties, so that we can decide together how to use Sophrology to serve them best. Some of my clients do not know anything about Sophrology before we start, so I often give them a brief explanation of what it is. I tell Daniel that the dynamic relaxation practice will help him find happiness and balance in his life, and give him the necessary tools to cope with every day and find a way to reach his potential in the future.

I explain how it will work: *'Sitting or standing with your eyes closed, I will guide you through a simple step-by-step practice that we have agreed on in advance, where you will take your body and mind into a state of relaxation while remaining alert. In this state, everything you experience and instruct yourself has a much greater impact on your consciousness and brings you to connect with your deep self. In this state of "dynamic relaxation", you move through a practice of simple breathing techniques, gentle movements, meditation and creative visualisation, and are encouraged to observe what you feel through your body and mind. Whether you are looking to manage your stress, prepare for events, find more well-being, confidence or positivity, or significantly transform your life, it is by repeating these simple practices that transformation will occur.*

Daniel had told me that he was struggling with his health, feeling weird sensations in his arms and a strong sense of oppression through his chest as a manifestation of his anxiety. With just one look at him I could see his body tension, his disconnection with the world around and his need to make changes before he reached a damaging burnout.

The Sophrology Practice

I knew that Daniel could use Sophrology to help his various issues – to reduce his stress and calm his anxiety, to give him back a sense of control over his life, to help him sleep and give him the strength to manage his emotional difficulties. And I knew that with just a few weeks of general

Sophrology practice, as I had experienced when I was just 15 years old, he would be able to transform his state of being and bring balance and increased happiness to his life.

We had agreed that the first and most pressing object-ive was to show him a simple and short Sophrology routine to help him relax and take a restorative pause in his daily life for both his body and mind. As our body goes into a 'fight or flight' state with stress, notably through stimulation of our nervous system and secreting specific hormones, practising Sophrology and breathing for 10 minutes a day helps reverse these effects as a first step into stress management.

After I had shown Daniel the exercises we were going to do, and he had agreed to them, I asked him to sit back in a reason-ably upright chair so that he could feel relaxed but without slumping in position, and we went straight into the exercises. Firstly, we looked at his breath and he started to practise centring its movement in the tummy rather than the chest.

Try this exercise yourself.

How Do You Breathe?

You can probably tell instinctively how relaxed your breath-ing is, but try this exercise to understand more about your breathing and how to 'listen' to it.

Sit comfortably in an upright chair, relaxed but not slumped.

Place one hand on the tummy area, around the belly button, and the other hand on the chest area over the breast-bone or sternum, and close your eyes.

Breathe in and out naturally a few times at first to establish your rhythm of breathing – do what feels natural rather than forcing your breathing through your nose or mouth in particular.

Now, notice the movement of your hands with the inhalation and exhalation. Do you feel motion in the chest and the tummy area, or just the upper part of the body?

Next, try to imagine that you have a balloon where your tummy is, and as you inhale the balloon grows bigger and when you exhale, it goes smaller. Sense the expansion and retraction as you inhale and exhale.

Make a note of your observations and then try this exercise again at a different part of the day and see if you notice a difference. Where is the movement: are you chest breathing or tummy breathing? 'Tummy breathing' is called deep breathing, belly breathing or diaphragmatic breathing, and is associated with numerous health benefits. The above exercise, coupled with other practices in the book, will slowly but surely help you reset your breath. If your breath is 'reversed', which means that you always breathe more from the chest than from the tummy, expect it to take some time to transform. It is often a deeply ingrained pattern that can reflect a physical, emotional or psychic state and shouldn't be forced to change. So start with noticing it rather than fighting it and things will naturally shift when your mind and body are ready through the practice.

After working with the breath for a few minutes, we used a simple Sophrology 'body scan' to support Daniel in reaching a deep state of relaxation called the 'sophroliminal state' (I explain this further on page 62), so he could restore his energy and connect with his body and physical sensation. Once in that state, he started to learn how to notice and listen to the tensions in his body, and we did an exercise called the Clearing Breath to release them (page 91), to help bring his body and mind into a happier place.

Tune into Your Body – The 'Tension Relax' Exercise

Now, how does reading Daniel's story make you feel? Does it make you feel tense and strained too? How did this show itself in your body and what did you feel? Try the following exercise to connect to your body:

Stand with your arms at your sides and breathe deeply a couple of times. Now, inhale and raise your arms up in front of you with your hands as fists. Now tense your entire body and hold the position for a couple of seconds. Then exhale and release the tension as you bring the arms back down to your sides. Take a moment to notice the sensation in your body. How do you feel different? Note any tension still in your body and acknowledge it. Tell it, 'I've seen you.' Repeat again.

This is a simple move to connect with the body and to let go of tension here and now. Practise it a couple of times each day to start to teach yourself to 'listen' to your body.

With Daniel, we finished with a short tailored practice to bring calm and relaxation through visualisation. The simple guided exercises allow the recipient to easily relax, efficiently clear their mind and therefore give space for a transformative or informative experience. No prior experience of any form of meditation, breathwork or posture-based therapies such as yoga are needed, but those who have practised meditation or mindfulness often find it easier to connect to their body, notice and let go of their tensions and reach a state of calm. And everyone responds differently to the practice – some even fall asleep!

The practice with Daniel lasted approximately 15 minutes and I recorded it as an audio file so that he could easily repeat it at home or at work until the next session. This first session would hopefully allow him to form his first transformative and restorative experience and allow me to find the best way to help him. Not everybody accesses relaxation or stilling the mind in the same way – for some, more movement is necessary before they can let go; for others, closing the eyes and doing the body scan will work. By practising the different exercises in this book, you will quickly realise what feels more natural or easier for you in order to reach a state of calm or to feel more grounded.

I asked Daniel to practise with the recording once a day, ideally during his lunch break or after work. I also gave him the two exercises outlined above to use throughout the day so he could regularly tune in and acknowledge how he felt as well as letting go of tensions or anxiety. The first one was simply to check his breath two or three times a day and notice where its movement was: was he chest breathing or tummy breathing? The second one was the simple tension relax exercise.

I knew that the observation of breathing and allowing it to be more abdominal would inform Daniel about his level of stress in the moment as well as helping him to calm down. The tension relax exercise would help him to sense his tensions on the spot, and take the time to acknowledge them and let them go. In a busy daily life, especially at work or busy with family, there is often very little time to acknowledge the tensions we feel. A few phone calls that leave us tense and frustrated, the pressure of a deadline, a colleague who drives us crazy or a sleepless night, and you are ready to explode at the smallest things, feeling achy in your body or simply exhausted. A regular practice of Sophrology will make a massive difference in knowing how to deal with these but it is sometimes just necessary to deal with it on the spot too. Instead of denying our state or blocking it out, a simple tension relax will allow us to connect with the tension we feel and consciously decide to let it go.

Think Less, Be More

In your daily life, are you fully present most of the time? Do you remember your journey to work or the school run this morning or were you thinking about a meeting you were having later in the day? Did you sit down and enjoy your meals fully today, or were you eating while working, driving or trying to do some online supermarket shopping? How much time do you spend thinking about your past or worrying about your future? How much of your day was spent in your head, and how much in your body? Most of us are familiar with the concept of living in the now, or mindful living, and its huge benefits that allow us to live life to the full, but do we really know how to achieve it?

For some of us, it feels uncomfortable to try to do less, to stop distracting ourselves with our phone or reading the news. Multi-tasking has become the norm, the expectation – as Daniel was experiencing. We desperately need more time to pause, more time to relax in our lives. Learning to connect to yourself and to tune into your daily life, even if it is just sitting on public transport or walking to your next meeting, will bring a huge sense of freedom and will release you from the pressure, allowing you to find more happiness and stability. Once you start practising Sophrology regularly over a few weeks, you will naturally be able to tune into a state of 'being' rather than 'doing' all the time as you go through your day, completing task after task. With regular short and simple practices (10 minutes a day is sufficient at the beginning), Sophrology is a gentle and efficient way to learn to be more present and happy in the current moment.

'*Before I started doing Sophrology, I just felt too much within myself – not just with tennis, but with life. I felt stressed all the time. But when I started using it, even after the first session, my whole outlook changed.*' Benjamin

As we practise Sophrology we start on this path to greater awareness. Regularly tuning in is the best way to recharge and feel inspired in our lives so that our actions become more meaningful. We have the power and innate ability to change the way we react and respond to present situations, and to change our relationship to our past and future. And by amending the way we feel, we affect the way we relate to others and how others treat us. We are breaking the cycle, which in turn brings opportunities and potential where we didn't see them before, preventing negative cycles of behaviour and response. When we are 'stuck' in life, we become 'unstuck', and when we are caught up in a vicious cycle of stress and pressure, we stop the behaviour and break free to create our own positive response.

And so what happened to Daniel? He came for six sessions of Sophrology and still finds the time to practise at home. By the end of his course with me, he was almost unrecognisable from the Daniel I had seen on that first day. His colour was normal, his energy levels were high in a very healthy way, he was sleeping well and had gained a greater clarity. He was making life choices to ensure that his state of being remained balanced and healthy, and he went away keen to tell others about how these simple practices had turned his life around.

Sophrology gives us the power to decide how we want to feel, and how we let the outside world affect us. Through Sophrology we can press a 'reset' button and live our lives with a new sense of perspective. Sophrology allows us to focus on what makes us happy and fulfilled, and gives us the gift to live a meaningful life guided by our own true self and our own core values.

Where is Sophrology From?

'And therefore if the head and body are to be
well, you must begin by curing the soul; that is
the first thing. For this' he said, 'is the great error
of our day in the treatment of the human body,
that physicians separate the soul from the body.'

PLATO BC 157

The term 'Sophrology' was created in 1960, inspired by
the word 'sophrosyne' used by Plato (meaning temper-
ance, tranquillity in thinking and acting as a way to find
harmony of body, mind and soul, or a state of healthy
soul). 'Sophrology' – *Sophrologie* in French – is taken
from the Greek words *Sos* (harmony), *Phren* (consciousness or spirit) and *Logos* (discourse, science, study).
Sophrology literally means 'the science of consciousness
in harmony'.

Alfonso Caycedo, a Spanish medical student born in
Colombia in 1932, wasn't yet qualified when he was
accepted to enter the service of Professor López Ibor, an

eminent psychiatrist in the Provincial Hospital of Madrid. Caycedo had the difficult and frequent task of giving electroshock treatment to and inducing insulinic comas in the mentally ill patients at the hospital. He was dismayed at how 'violent' these controversial methods were and he queried: 'Why does consciousness have to be shaken in order to heal?' He realised that the medical world at the time knew very little about consciousness/ awareness, although it was fundamental to human existence. He believed it was essential to understand it better to come up with new and kinder therapeutic processes to deal with depression and mental illness, and he thought more research was needed into how to access consciousness.

In 1960, he created the term 'Sophrologie' and its first clinical department in that same Madrid hospital, with the firm intention of developing new therapeutic processes. He was already studying the work of the esteemed German psychotherapist, Johannes Heinrich Schultz, who devised a world-famous system of self-hypnosis called autogenic training, and the German philosopher Edmund Husserl, who founded the study of phenomenology.

Phenomenology

Caycedo rightly pointed out that phenomenology is very complex, and it is not the intention of this book to understand all of it. What is important here is how it relates to the philosophy and practice of Sophrology. Phenomenology in its broadest sense is the study of the structures of experience and consciousness – that is, the 'phenomena' of how we experience things. In Sophrology we use it to feel, note and observe what is happening during our practice (the phenomena emerging from our consciousness) and later what is happening outside the practice, in our daily life, without interpreting or transforming it. We remain as non-judgemental as possible, without preconceived ideas of what these phenomena are or mean. In this way, phenomenology supports a way of discovering the essence of everything.

Professor López Ibor became a mentor to Caycedo in his research and advised him to go to Switzerland to meet Professor Ludwig Binswanger, a leading psychiatrist using existential phenomenology as a therapeutic approach. Caycedo's time in Switzerland taught him a lot about this approach to mental illness, but did not give him the practical therapeutic tools he was looking for to help his patients.

Binswanger then advised him to study consciousness in its healthy states, and go to the East to learn about the vast tradition of knowledge the yogis have, acquired through their ancient techniques and practices, to access higher states of consciousness. From 1965, he spent two years working with doctors and yogis in Delhi and all over India. He wanted to learn the different approaches they had and he studied their practices – the power of breathing and bodywork – to transform consciousness. He realised the importance of the practical element in complementing the theoretical or philosophical principles of phenomenology he had researched. In Dharamsala, he met with the Dalai Lama and studied Tibetan Buddhism. He then visited Japan to study the principles of Zen meditation. His aim was to find gentle ways to improve the daily lives of his patients.

Caycedo's Influences:

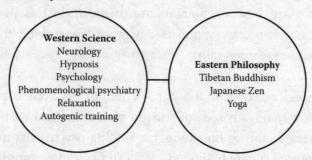

Western Science
Neurology
Hypnosis
Psychology
Phenomenological psychiatry
Relaxation
Autogenic training

Eastern Philosophy
Tibetan Buddhism
Japanese Zen
Yoga

Returning to Spain and settling in Barcelona, he developed the first levels of the Sophrology practice, also called the Caycedo Dynamic Relaxation. This beautifully blends the Western science of consciousness with principles of yoga, Buddhist meditation and Japanese Zen, from the presence of the physical body in yoga to the use of contemplation and sound, in order to reach more balance in consciousness.

He clinically tested the techniques on private clients and on patients in the *Sophrologie* and *Psychosomatique* departments in the Barcelona hospital. Caycedo made sure that the unique and accessible techniques were adapted to the Western lifestyle, and that they would answer the specific concerns of his patients, working to reduce stress, decrease anxiety, improve sleep and promote positivity. In the late 1960s, Caycedo was appointed Professor at the Barcelona Faculty of Medicine and, for the next two decades, he continued to research and develop the full 12 Levels of Sophrology, and to teach his methods throughout Europe, especially in Switzerland and France, as well as in his native Colombia.

Meeting Alfonso Caycedo

When I decided to train to become a Caycedian Sophrologist, I knew that I wanted to train with Alfonso Caycedo. I remember feeling a mix of huge excitement and worry about meeting him. What if the man whose teachings I had followed for so long over the foundation years of my life was not quite my cup of tea? What if his teachings were not the same as I had learnt and practised?

When I finally attended my first lecture with him, I discovered someone totally dedicated to his creation, who really believed in the infinite resource that is consciousness. A highly scientific researcher, fully grounded but who was also able to see beyond, to bring his vision to the world. He was very courteous and I found that his eyes were a mix of mystery and gentleness, the mystery that you often find in those whose life has given them a kind of wisdom. Being guided by the person at the source of the method was an amazing experience, and I feel very fortunate to have crossed his path.

As I was writing this book the sad news came that he had passed away, and it is his deeply resonating voice that will stay with me. I am eternally grateful to him for profoundly changing my life for the better through his method and his teachings. I have no doubt that his work will continue to spread and inspire future generations.

Sophrology Now

Over 50 years later, Sophrology has become a global phenomenon and hugely relevant in today's modern world. Though created for the medical sphere, Caycedo's methods quickly reached a wider audience. They were first adapted to numerous medical specialities (oncology, obstetrics, cardiology and palliative care), to improve the well-being of patients or in the prevention of disease, and then quickly spread to the worlds of education, sports science and stress management.

In Europe, Sophrology is currently used in many different areas of life and health. It is often offered in maternity units and practised by midwives to help prepare for birth and positive pregnancy experiences. It is also offered for those undergoing IVF treatment. It is particularly popular in specialist sleep units across Europe to treat sleep disorders and insomnia. And it is of course used to great effect in private practice and clinics for stress management.

As a 'dynamic relaxation' technique, Sophrology has also been taught over the years to prepare for major events – in corporate environments before important presentations, and in schools to help teenagers to prepare for exams (where it is also taught for improving confidence, concentration and to help develop positive attitudes). Sophrology is frequently used in the business sector to improve employees' focus, confidence and well-being, and is such a well-known overall health technique that it is paid for by most private health insurances in France and Switzerland.[1]

Sophrology has spread to such a degree that there are now over 100 schools of Sophrology in France alone. Famous sportspeople who have benefited from Sophrology range from Olympic swimmers to skiing champions and tennis stars, such as Yannick Noah. The world-famous Spanish golfer, Seve Ballesteros, studied with Caycedo. He spoke about how he would practise Sophrology in the bathroom before a tournament started, and how it helped him to increase his self-belief and motivation, and to find more meaning in his playing, stating: 'I have studied Sophrology and firmly believe that I owe my success to Sophrology.' [*]

Professor Alfonso Caycedo retired in 2007, and his daughter Natalia Caycedo, also a Doctor in psychiatry, is

[*] *Sophrologie Caycédienne* magazine, issue 65, 2011

continuing his work. What began as one man's passion to ease the distress of patients suffering severe mental illness has become a practice that can transform the daily life of millions of people around the world.

As Little or as Much as You Want: The 12 Levels

Caycedo devised 12 Levels for the full Sophrology method, each level with a set of specific exercises and aims. They are organised into three cycles: Levels 1–4 are the Discovery Cycle, Levels 5–8 are the Mastery Cycle and Levels 9–12 are the Transformative Cycle (we focus on the first cycle here in this book). Although working through the 12 Levels (which are generally completed over a period of at least two years) allows a deeper and more permanent level of transformation, every time you close your eyes and practise, Sophrology allows you to have a meaningful experience and an opportunity to find more harmony, balance and happiness. The Levels are a framework or a structure for experiences that will naturally support transformation, meeting you where you are and taking you where your consciousness is ready to go. They allow you to explore and uncover progressive aspects of consciousness, going deeper into what Caycedo called the 'unveiling of consciousness'.

The 12 Levels journey is ordered in the way it has been built to allow you to discover, master and transform consciousness. Each Level has its intention and aim. This journey allows your awareness to expand, transforming the way you see and relate to yourself and the world around you. The experience and transformation you gain from this journey is different for everyone, but it will certainly help you to become free from limiting beliefs, give you a chance to better comprehend where you come from and where you are going, and enable you to more clearly define who you are and to find a life that meets that true self. Caycedo also created 40 Specific Techniques, which have been enriched by other Sophrologists along the way, to address the specific needs of the individual.

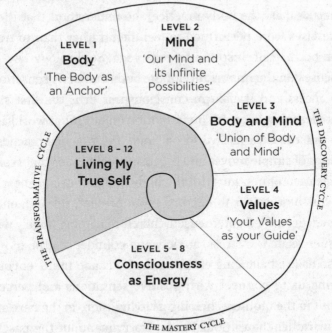

Some of this may look complicated to the newcomer as you read, but don't worry – Sophrology is first and foremost a guided practice, and these steps take all their meaning when you actually feel them rather than try to make sense of them with just your mind. For the first steps into the practice, you will be given all the basic principles and tools to be confident in learning and benefiting from the method.

Level 1: The Body as an Anchor

When Caycedo was in India, studying the way yogis perform their asanas (the body practice), he understood that these exercises were performed to feel them rather than to train the body itself. Inspired by Raja yoga, Sophrology Level 1 focuses on the importance of the body and body sensations to access and transform consciousness. It is the first step into learning to centre our attention on our inner world and to put the external world on hold. The practice teaches a series of simple moves and breathing techniques that create a clearer connection with the body in our consciousness. It helps the receiver to become more present, relaxed, energised, grounded and focused, therefore helping hugely with issues related to stress, anxiety and confidence. The moves also have a balancing effect on the body and mind, encouraging us to connect with positive sensations and perceptions in the moment, helping us to live more in the here and now rather than in our heads, worrying about the past or the future. The Specific Techniques of Level 1 will also focus on helping with particular issues such as building confidence, learning to find calm and giving access to instant serenity.

Level 2: Our Mind and its Infinite Possibilities

Inspired by Tibetan meditation, Level 2 concentrates on the mind and the discovery of its infinite possibilities. Caycedo realised that a lot of the Eastern methods to free the mind used contemplation. We are not talking about the contemplation of a divinity (like in the religious practice Caycedo observed) but rather a passive contemplation that consists in noting a presence; we are learning to note the presence of our body, our mind and our senses. Using simple sitting practices and visualisations, Level 2 encourages us to focus and note our perceptions. It reinforces our ability to concentrate, imagine, to be creative, and perform better with increased focus. It helps us accept our present and build a positive and creative outlook on our future, including ways to prepare for events using positive visualisations (e.g. for exams, speeches, birth or surgery).

Level 3: Union of Body and Mind

With its origins in Japanese Zen, the practice of Level 3 allows a deeper connection between the mind and body and teaches us how to live through that connection. It allows us to amend emotional patterns from the past to enable us to live a better present and gives us the power to transform our present and future. This is a natural progression of the previous 2 Levels and, in order to feel this deeper connection, takes a little more practice. Here, we have the opportunity to revisit our past looking for the positives, notably using visualisation.

Level 4: Our Values as Our Guide

Level 4 shows us how to identify our personal values and stimulate their presence within us. Now that we have a stronger centre through the first 3 Levels, we are more acquainted with our body and mind, as well as recognising their deep link. From here we can explore what values guide our daily actions and aspirations. The practice of Level 4, including exercises where our eyes are open, and even walking meditations, will support us in finding greater meaning in our daily living and to trust ourselves to find a more meaningful life according to our own personal values. It will also help us to realise that present, past and future are one, enabling us to reinforce our ability to stay in the present moment and enjoy it for what it is.

Levels 5–12 are packed with lovely, simple practices that will guide you to explore further the infinite aspect of consciousness and give you access to deeper layers of your consciousness. It is not the purpose of this book to go into great depth on these Levels, but they teach us to be our own alchemists and will deeply transform the way we relate to ourselves and others, making us more authentic to who we truly are. (See page 42 for more details on the 12 Levels.)

As you will discover Sophrology is a vast subject, with its own specific language and structure, notably in the way practical exercises are guided and ordered. For this book, I have selected the exercises and information I found most accessible and relevant for the reader (even if some of the exercises are not part of Caycedian Sophrology). I have also translated and sometimes adapted the specific terminology of Sophrology from French here to ensure the meaning is kept and to allow you to engage fully with the exercises. My hope is that we can all feel and connect to the true Life-Changing Power of Sophrology!

How to Use this Book

The joy of Sophrology is that it is a guided practice and it requires no specialist knowledge, equipment or clothing. So, beginning your journey with Sophrology is just a matter of you, a space that is relatively quiet (don't let your environment stop you if you need to practise with the children in the room), 10 minutes' spare time and ideally an upright chair – such as a dining chair. Then just put in your earphones or start up your computer and listen to my voice. Throughout the book, I'll tell you when you get to the downloadable guided exercises with an icon like this ◁)). They are downloadable from my website: www.be-sophro.com/the-life-changing-power-of-sophrology.

Everything in this book will make more sense once you have done a week of daily practice. For those who want to understand the depth of the method, you can carry on reading the book in order. For those who are keen to practise straight away, then just move to the Foundation Practice.

For your practice, I recommend you:
Start with the three key techniques of the **Foundation Practice** (page 74) for the first 5–7 days so that your body and your mind have time to get used to the beginning of the

Sophrology method to reach the sophroliminal state of consciousness and release tensions. Perform each proposed stage of the Foundation Practice three or four times so that you become confident with its steps.

Then:
Move to the **15 Minutes to Balance Your Body and Mind** section of this book (page 108), which comes in **two parts** so that you can do a full practice (30 minutes) or split it over two sessions. This Level 1 practice alone is a life-changing practice with a wide range of benefits, from stress management to increased confidence, and higher energy levels to improved resilience as you learn to deepen your connection between body and mind.

Or:
Look at the **10 Minutes to Change Your Daily Life** section of this book (page 128) to discover how to use Sophrology for specific goals. This is where you will be able to deepen your practice and create 'on the go' tools to grant you instant calm, serenity, confidence and focus.

Once you have explored some or all of these practices, in **10 Minutes to Build Your Positive Future** (page 175) you have the chance to shape your future and open up your full potential – for happiness and for change. Do take your time on the full Foundation Practice and Level 1 too though – the more practice and repetition of the basic exercises you do, the more your body will embrace the power of Sophrology.

'On the Go'

Throughout the book, I show you how Sophrology is a method that you can use anywhere, anytime. Once you have practised the basics, the supertools become exercises to be used to bring calm and clarity, confidence and motivation to your life wherever you are – in a meeting, before an important phone call, in the middle of a stressful interaction with a family member. Once Sophrology is part of your life, your mind and body work together to create new pathways to your new way of thinking.

Repetition, repetition, repetition

The practice was created so that you can include it in your daily life. It may be hard to find those 10 minutes each day, but a short regular practice is far better than 45 minutes once a week. To find out more, read on. Or, if you wish, find a chair and be guided into the experience of Sophrology straight away!

PART 2

Practising Sophrology

CASE STUDY: **BEATRICE** – *'I FELT COMPLETELY DISCONNECTED.'*

Beatrice has been practising Sophrology for two months within my BeSophro group – a group session I run where people come to learn new tools to address stress issues or to try Sophrology for the first time. Originally from the US, she lived in France and Germany before settling in the UK. She found Sophrology when researching ways to treat her postnatal depression, alongside talking therapy.

I had a baby last year and the district nurse told me three weeks after birth that I had postnatal depression. And I thought, 'No, I'm just being dramatic, there's nothing wrong with me.' So unfortunately it went untreated for a good six months after that. And it got to the point where it was hard to cope, even to wake up each day and see friends and inter-act with people. And then I had a few scary moments when I was unintentionally doing things that could hurt me. I think the worst incident was when I was crossing a road to go to a work meeting and I kind of just walked in front of a car. And the person had to swerve to avoid me. And then I realised that this was serious and I needed to address how I was feeling. I felt completely disconnected from my body – disconnected from who I used to be, who I wanted to be.

Everything felt out of sync so I went to the doctor and they confirmed that I had a really bad case of postnatal depression. And they sent me to a psychiatrist and he had a load of pills. I didn't want to take them. I tried them but one of them that was supposed to make me sleep just made me feel not with it all day long. And I didn't think that was acceptable, so I started to look around for alternative ways to manage it in conjunction with my talking therapy and medication. And by some miracle an interview with Dominique on a new mums' blog popped up. And so I read all about it in French, because what I saw in English was very vague. If more people knew about it I think more people would recommend it for postnatal depression. I joined one of the group sessions to see what it was all about. At that point I had nothing to lose. I just loved the session. At the end I felt better than I had in a really long time. I felt I was starting to get back in touch with myself. And that's been my experience so far.

You realise that it is not some big grand zen-with-the-world feeling. I felt like something was going – that numb sensation. I think what I learnt that first session was how to relax properly – how to tune out the outside and start focusing inwards and on what was in myself. It felt really important to have that moment to tune out all you can hear in your mind and all the noise outside. And the first few exercises did their job just helping me with techniques for when I'm stressed – to stop and pause and focus. That's the biggest thing I got out of the first session.

As we were doing the visualisation exercises I found it quite easy to hold the images in my mind of positivity and what I envisaged. When an outside thought came in I had to force myself to really focus like I had at the beginning. And once I did that I really felt quite free, and it's been a long time since I felt that kind of freedom in myself. And freedom to express myself to myself. When a lot of the time we're very busy turning off the noise of ourselves we lose our true intentions and sense of what our purpose is.

Talking to friends, I described it as feeling 'like I was blocked and I wasn't connecting with myself'. I felt that Sophrology basically gave me a safe environment with positive energy for me to release, learn how to focus and search internally for the answer that I need to . . . really evaluate myself in a non-judgemental way. People say that's really fascinating.

The Five Powers to Unlock Your Potential

The way that most of us live these days doesn't encourage or allow us the space and time to be present in and connected to our bodies. We usually only start to pay attention to our body when it is achy, painful, blocked, tired or sick. We can actually feel betrayed and let down by the fact that it suddenly won't do what we want it to and that we are forced to stop and heal. Do you ever think of a headache as a signal to listen so that once you've ruled out anything serious, you can start thinking in a different way? Could the headache be a sign that you're dehydrated or struggling to process an emotional difficulty? Or do you find yourself annoyed because you need to finish an assignment so you take some painkillers and carry on? It's easy to just keep carrying on and 'doing' until your body reaches a state of burnout or serious breakdown and you can't carry on any longer.

Sophrology looks to fix that disconnection, and direct the power of our consciousness to where we need greater strength in our life. In this chapter, we look at the five core pillars of Sophrology that support the practice: the body and mind, the sophroliminal state, the breath, movement and stillness, and positive intention. It's helpful to understand a little more about how Sophrology has the effect that it does.

1. The Body and Mind

It's difficult to overstate the power of the physical body in Sophrology. We might not feel as if we can rip off our clothes to reveal a superhero outfit underneath, but we have lost the knowledge of the innate ability and wisdom of our bodies.

Sophrology teaches us to feel the importance of our bodies as our anchor in living our life and as the reservoir of all our inner resources. All our emotions, thoughts, beliefs, capacities and experiences are stored in the body as consciousness, which is one of the reasons why listening to our body through sensation is so crucial. By developing a deeper connection with and increasing the awareness of our body, we gain a powerful access to our true self and potential for transformation as a way through life's stresses and problems.

Sensation

Using the body alongside the mind in a dynamic way in order to heal is one of the key strengths of and differences between Sophrology and other mindfulness techniques – and the key to Level 1 of Sophrology. As you rapidly learn to connect with your body sensations through the practice of simple moves, you give your body the opportunity to show you how it feels. If you have been under extreme tension for a period of time, that initial experience might include you first becoming aware of these tensions. It is common for my clients to tell me: 'I had not noticed how much tension I had in my shoulders', or to realise how little they have awareness of certain regions of their body, like the tummy for example. We will talk a lot about 'sensation' in Sophrology. Without trying to analyse them, you will observe any feelings of warmth, tension, tightness or lightness in the various parts of your body. Once we get to the Foundation Practice, we'll look at exactly how you note or record what you experience during the practice – called the 'vivance' in Sophrology. This can be the sensations that you felt in your body, along with any perceptions that came to you during the exercises and whether or not you struggled to follow the practice, and to focus. It's helpful and illuminating to keep a record of the vivance in what in Sophrology we call the phenodescription (page 84).

'With stress, you cut off and disconnect. You end up in your head a lot, which is what happened to me. My understanding of stress is that it's not just your mind, it's your body too. There is a physiological approach – the "fight or flight" response – and as much as doing something like meditation helps, it's really difficult with your heart pounding in flight mode. But in Sophrology it's about the body too, you're doing things.' Catherine

As we develop our practice, every time we connect with the body in Sophrology we also connect with the mind.

They are a unit and the aim is to make that connection stronger so that we are more unified and in tune with our whole consciousness. Try this exercise to see the mind–body connection in practice.

The Mind–Body Link Exercise

This will just take a minute. Begin by sitting upright and comfortable with your eyes closed.

Place one hand on your tummy and the other hand on the central chest area, and close your eyes.

Breathe in and out a few times and establish your natural pattern of relaxed breathing.

Now, visualise something positive and joyful – think about your best friend or your last holiday, your pet or your favourite place – something that makes you feel happy and relaxed.

Now observe how your body feels. Do you feel relaxed or tense, and where is the tension? Does your body feel 'open' or 'closed'? Notice if your breath has changed.

Then think of something sad or uncomfortable – it can be something you heard on a news report or something currently causing you stress in your life.

Again, feel for tension in your body and any sensation. Notice your breathing.

And finally, return to the pleasant image that you created first. Notice any change in your body.

If you're not sure you can feel anything, it doesn't matter. Take a couple more minutes to tune into your body. Look for the positive sensations that you might have felt. Notice how much easier it is to listen to negative sensation – discomfort, tension, pain and heaviness. Note how your mind directly influences your body.

Positive Somatisation

We all know that pain is an important signal from the body to alert us to danger, a protection mechanism so that we can react accordingly. But we are not good at more subtle feelings, or at cultivating the positive. We need to look at sensation in a different way.

How we experience life has a strong influence on our physical self. Now think of all the stress that we can experience on even a good day – the simple pressures of fitting in everything that we need to get done, responding to a multitude of people and problems and ticking off things on our to-do list – and therefore over how much of each day our body and our breathing are impacted.

This pathway of somatisation – the appearance of psychological issues in physical symptoms – is used in reverse within Sophrology. Instead of letting negative events impact on our body we create a positive somatisation by using all our resources of mind and body, and our vital power, to help calm the mind and keep both in balance. By focusing on what feels healthy, happy, comfortable and confident, we use our mind–body connection to shift our whole self towards a more positive state.

....

*'All positive actions on one part of our consciousness
will reverberate on the totality of our Being.'**

ALFONSO CAYCEDO

....

Caycedo's States of Consciousness

When Caycedo created his method in 1960, he came up with one of its fundamental principles: the different states of consciousness. When we look at consciousness in Sophrology it can be in several qualitative states. Caycedo describes three of them as: 'normal', 'pathological' and 'sophronique'. Normal is the ordinary state of consciousness, where the individual lives in its natural state, without questioning its reality. Pathological is when the state of consciousness is altered or disrupted by disease (for example – with depression, psychosis, neurosis or dementia). And 'sophronique' is the state of consciousness we aim for with the practice of Sophrology: a pure state of harmony and balance of body, mind and soul.

---

* *'Toute action positive sur une partie de la conscience se répercute sur la totalité de l'être.'*

2. The Sophroliminal State

With the practice of Sophrology, we can easily learn to reach a different level of vigilance, called the sophroliminal state. With a simple body scan, we are guided into a state where the body is relaxed and the mind is alert. We are not hypnotised or close to sleeping. Rather, we are in a state of relaxed clarity that allows us to connect with consciousness more directly than when we are in our normal getting-on-with-life state.

Effectively, in the sophroliminal state, we are in a state in between waking and sleeping, more traditionally called the alpha brainwave state. In this state – unlike some deep hypnotic states – you remain conscious throughout your practice and in control of the process. You will be able to recall and give an account of all the sensations, feelings and perceptions you have experienced in that state in your phenodescription. You are focused on the present and able to 'view' situations and emotions with less judgement or less attached emotion.

Not only is it a lovely and relaxing state to be in, but it has been scientifically proven* to be a state where your body heals, where your nervous system can rest, and your mind can relax. This sophroliminal state is the gateway to connect with your consciousness and your inner resources. It is the optimal brain state for positively programming mind and body and in which you can

* www.ncbi.nlm.nih.gov/pubmed/22700446 and www.mountsinai. org/about-us/newsroom/press-releases/systems-biology-research-study-reveals-benefits-of-vacation-and-meditation

directly access memory, imagination, creativity, vitality and intuition. It helps you to reset deep-seated beliefs and understanding and to build inner resources such as confidence, joy, motivation and recuperation – you are in your 'gentle superpower zone'.

'I really enjoyed the relaxation method that put us into the sophroliminal state. I realised that I can easily calm myself down or re-energise myself without having to sleep or take a long break.' Richard

The practice of Sophrology can't happen without diving into that sophroliminal state, but as you will notice over time, practising regularly will allow you to connect with this state very quickly. It will become more and more available in your daily life as and when you need it.

3. The Breath

Scientists and practitioners from all areas of health happily agree on the power of breathing to affect our mental and physical health – both in the short term and over a longer period. The breath and how to use it to affect body and mind is a huge subject on its own. By all means, go out and buy a book about breathing and learn more about it, but Sophrology doesn't require such extensive knowledge or practice.

Yoga sees the breath as the source of *prana*, our vital force and the doorway between the conscious and unconscious. In osteopathy, it is viewed from a more mechanical point of view – an osteopath will make sure that the mechanical action of the diaphragm is as free as possible in relation to the organs surrounding it so that oxygen, blood nutrients, lymph and all fluids can circulate freely to ensure optimal function and to promote good health.

Observe your breathing as it changes constantly throughout the day – from the first moments on waking up in a relaxed state, to perhaps an early panic about finding a clean pair of trousers, followed by a caffeine hit with your first coffee of the day, followed by a brisk journey to work or the school run – perhaps along a busy and fume-filled road. Our breathing and oxygen levels are constantly responding to our activities, our emotions and thoughts, our energy levels and our environment. Try the How Do You Breathe? exercise again (page 27).

'Just to close your eyes and connect with your breathing shows you how tense you are. Most of the time you don't know that you're so tense.' Penelope

When we are under pressure, our breathing naturally becomes fast and shallow and more centred in the chest – part of the 'fight or flight' response. In some circumstances this is a crucial response from the body, but at other times it is most definitely not helpful. But the reverse is also true – deeper breathing using our tummy increases and supports the relaxation of the nervous system and the muscles, and helps to calm the mind.

In Sophrology, we use the breath as a way in to the power

of consciousness: breathing to increase awareness, to reach the relaxed sophroliminal state, and therefore to access our superpowers. The breath is a bridge between the mind and the body, a doorway to consciousness and a way to connect to the here and now, to the sensations as they are, without analysis or judgement. Every time you close your eyes and breathe, you are connecting with your being.

In the practice, we usually aim to breathe in and out through the nose. Occasionally a practitioner might ask someone new to Sophrology to breathe out through the mouth in order to be able to observe their breathing, to ensure that they are not holding their breath in their early practice and to help them to focus on their breathing. See what is easier and most comfortable for you during your practice.

The Calming Breath

In The Calming Breath exercise, we are also using the mouth to exhale so we can lengthen the out breath as much as possible. We are aiming for a 'tummy breath' rather than chest breathing to encourage relaxation and calm. It's important to remember though that this is not about forcing the breath to change, it's about getting to know your breath through the practice, and trusting that it will naturally change over time. Try this exercise to lengthen the breath:

Take a normal and deep breath in through the nose and then out through the mouth several times.

Now, count the length of your in breath and breathe out to twice the length, so in for 3 counts and out for 6, or if you are an experienced deep breather, then in for 5 and out for a count of 10. Imagine that you are slowly blowing out a candle with the out breath.

Repeat this mindfully for 2–3 minutes with your eyes closed. You will notice after a while that the body and mind calm down.

Using Your Breath with Intention

There are many different ways of breathing to influence your physical body and nervous system in order to calm, ground or even energise you through oxygenation. In the practice, we couple the breath with a specific intention, thought or movement to connect with our inner resources. Often we use the breath as a way to stimulate our vital power of, for example, confidence or calm, or to connect with a positive sensation on the spot. It is also a powerful tool to release tensions and negative thoughts, as you will see in the Foundation Practice.

We can also use the breath to calm ourselves down, as in the exercise above.

4. Movement and Stillness

In the first levels of Sophrology, we use a combination of simple standing movements and short periods of stillness or pause in the practice. Movements are called **activations**

– they create more sensation for us to observe. Activations can also take the form of breathing, a particular posture or a visualisation.

Activations are usually followed by a pause, called an **integration pause**. An integration pause is simply a time where we note and observe our sensations and take the time to let them integrate or register deeper in our body and mind. Taking that time to pause and just be is a key part of the practice of Sophrology – perhaps the most important, as this is when the true work within takes place. It can take only a few seconds or up to a minute or more, and it is something that we use between steps in the practice. I like to think of the integration as a stage almost like a snowstorm ornament – having shaken up our consciousness, we now let everything settle and re-organise again. The power of the simple pause should not be underestimated. It is greatly beneficial in increasing focus and concentration and in learning to be this non-judgemental observer of our inner world. It teaches us to meditate.

The alternance of stillness and movement is one of the core strengths of Sophrology and a brilliant way of helping even the most resistant to relax and learn to meditate. I have had many clients who are so agitated and stressed that asking them to sit and focus on their breathing for 5 minutes is simply not possible. It would make them feel even more tense, and give them the impression that this is simply something they can't do. With Sophrology, you have the options of movements to release the tensions so that people can be gently guided into stiller practice only when they are ready. It is the art of the Sophrologist to understand what will work with a client and how the method can be tailored to specific needs.

I find that the combination of action and pause is also a very therapeutic way to relearn that we cannot be efficient for 24 hours each day, and that we actually have to learn to pause. The brain and body need that.

5. The Positive Intention

And the final piece of the Sophrology puzzle is the power of intention, a very powerful resource that we use in our Sophrology practice. As you know, Sophrology is a tool that serves many purposes and can help with a wide variety of issues. Sometimes the same exercises will be valid for numerous issues and often, if not always, it is useful to be clear on the goal we want to achieve before starting our practice, as well as learning to be open to all possibilities and revelations while we are practising. Each level has its specific aim but it's also necessary to be clear on your purpose before you start your practice. Some days you will need calm; on other days you will need to stimulate your energy or confidence. From experience, I can tell you that your consciousness listens and knows, and will guide you towards what you need to achieve that goal or reach the state you wish to be in. Things will shift and move in your life because of it.

Bring your trust to your practice, persevere and let go – and enjoy what is to come.

Positive Intention Suggestions

What is it that you wish to achieve with the day's practice? Are you looking to feel calmer, more centred, or to let go? Are you getting ready for an important day or do you need to perform to your best ability? Are you looking for answers in relation to decisions you need to make?

All of the following can be part of your practice through your intention: calm, resilience, warmth, light, focus, joy, happiness, confidence, concentration, security, comfort, positivity, relaxation, self-belief, trust, freedom, serenity, peace, grounding, reassurance. Your consciousness will help guide you in your choice.

As you are raising your energy to another level, notice what happens outside your practice, in your daily life, in relation to the intention you have set. You may be surprised to discover that answers and solutions come to you, maybe in the form of what people tell you, an article you are reading or a new job opportunity. Remaining open and non-judgemental inside and outside your practice will open a new world of possibilities.

Repeating the practice will help you reach your goals and strengthen your resources, and along the way it will also form part of your journey of self-discovery. Enjoy!

CASE STUDY: **PENELOPE**
– 'FOR WHEN YOUR MIND
GOES OUT OF CONTROL.'

Penelope, 43, was a nurse in a large London hospital at the time she started Sophrology – burnt out by the constant stress of providing the best care in a hugely pressured and demanding environment and the desire to help others at any price. She had a common trait of those who are passionate, highly competent and perfectionist about what they do, and exceptional at their work: she was unable to take account of her own needs. She came to Sophrology as she was on the verge of a breakdown. She had been signed off work and put on medication by a psychiatrist. While she was talking with her psychiatrist about her work problems and issues from her background, what she wanted and needed were practical tools to help her cope with her situation.

I used Sophrology when it was the worst time of my life. I was not coping with my work and since it was my passion I felt trapped and could not find the way out. My mind and my body were constantly overloaded. I had to see a psychiatrist because I had cried for 48 hours nonstop. I met my Sophrologist and just said, 'Please help me. I can't sleep and I can't go back to work as I can't take it any more.'

As I was a very efficient and in control person it was so traumatic to feel that way. I felt as if I could not give what people expected of me – I felt very guilty to be weak. And I was punishing myself for that too. I felt guilty for my colleagues as they were really busy and I felt guilty for leaving as I'm sure they didn't realise it was really bad, they thought I was coping OK. The medical environment is very stressful. The doctors and medical staff decide things and sometimes you don't have a choice. And people would ask me to do things and I needed to say no but I wasn't able to. I felt so unprotected and couldn't take any more. I knew it was all in my head but I felt dangerous.

My Sophrologist just said, 'It's not a problem, we'll find a way.' And she 'put me back' into my body. I remember that the first thing she did was to teach me to create this safe space – this bubble (page 135) – a protection technique like a filter so that all the stress and noise couldn't get to me. I had felt so unprotected and couldn't take any more. Then she made me breathe for a while, and then jump up and down for a few moments at a time and do a walking exercise just to make me come back down into my body. She told me that I needed to visualise what I wanted. We drew some circles, and in the middle we put all the things that I could do, showing me my inner resources. And I could see that in 15 minutes just breathing under her guidance and feeling protected from everything in my head changed me. We did a recording in the session so that I could just plug in later and I had exercises that I could do everywhere. And the effect in one hour was just so powerful. This was life beginning again, a new chapter.

When I left, I was walking and I felt present and better attached to the ground. And my mind was relieved. I felt a bit stoned, like after the dentist. She really helped me to release the pressure inside my head, like a boiling pan. I had felt that my life was over. And after just one hour – everyone asked me what I had taken! For my personality it was brilliant. I think everyone should have these tools – you know, for when your mind goes out of control.

It's more about noticing when your mind takes over and grounding myself and connecting to my body sensation. When there's a cycle in my head of all the thoughts, I try to just breathe in and breathe out and when I do that I do a gesture with my hand and I consciously let it all go. It helps me to understand that we can have pressure, we can have stress. But if there's too much I can just take it down to zero and then I can go again. Right at the time – you're able to do that because you do Sophrology. You know what it feels like. At the moment, I don't feel tense, but I take the time to connect to my body.

Afterwards you feel as if your mind is more clear, as if you can see the rest of your story. My head was stuck and I could not get out of it, but I realised that I could have a different control of and perspective about my life through my body.

A few months later, I feel more empowered. If I wake up and feel lousy, I stand in front of my window, go inside my body and do some conscious breathing, and maybe The Bellows exercise (page 117). If you help your mind to go on something else and direct your breathing, and you add something you want – your intention – that's how it works. It's not magic, it's just how it works.

It's like my life is taking on a different rhythm. I trust again – it was such an extreme moment for me. Now I have enthusiasm and energy and a vision for the future. I've decided to retrain to become an independent nurse, so that I can control my hours and have a closer relationship with individual patients.

10 Minutes to Step into the Method:
The Foundation Practice

And now we begin our Sophrology journey!

The Foundation Practice is the starting point of the Sophrology programme and the root of all your Sophrology practice. These initial key techniques are the exercises you will go through in some form at the beginning of each practice in this book. You will repeat them at the start of whatever Sophrology level you practise, and whether you are doing a quick 10-minute practice in your bedroom or a longer session with a practitioner.

They form a simple way to anchor yourself in the present through sensation, to deeply connect your mind and body together and to take yourself into the 'relaxed alert' state of awareness, the sophroliminal state – making yourself ready and receptive for the full practice.

'I have this ritual every morning now. Being able to connect every morning makes me aware of my body and once I am there I can truly relax.' Maguelonne

And the great thing is that while this is the foundation for Sophrology, it is also an excellent relaxation, recuperation and stress-management tool in itself, as well as a simple way to start building positivity within consciousness. If you did no other Sophrology than this simple practice several times each week for two weeks, you would feel calmer, happier and more focused in your daily life.

The 5 Systems

As you are guided through firstly the Foundation Practice and the supertools of Sophrology, you will notice that your attention will be brought to the body by grouping its elements into what Sophrology calls the **5 Systems**. The 5 Systems 'map' the body to support body awareness by giving us the possibility to explore our body's individual parts with precision but also as a united structure. In Sophrology, we don't limit the body to its anatomy: each system is also a way into consciousness.

As you bring your awareness to each of the 5 Systems during the practice, you will quickly be able to locate possible tensions or blockages and use your breath or movement to release the tensions. You will begin to feel the energy flow of the systems and learn to contemplate or tune into their infinite resources, becoming aware that confidence, joy, vitality or motivation, for example, are not only of the mind but something we also feel deep in our bodies.

Body region	Areas covered	Centre of region or integration point
System 1	Head, brain and face	Point between the eyebrows
System 2	Neck, throat, shoulders, arms and hands	Position of thyroid gland – centre of the throat
System 3	Chest, upper back, breasts, heart and lungs	Breastbone
System 4	Stomach and upper digestive system, liver, kidneys and lower back	Upper tummy area, just below ribcage
System 5	Lower abdominal area, bladder, lower digestive tract, sexual organs, pelvic floor, hips, legs and feet	Below the belly button (between belly button and pelvic bone)
Megasystem	Entire body	On the belly button

(For ease in this book, I will be working with the arms as part of System 2, whereas in Caycedian Sophrology they are part of System 2 and System 3.)

Each system has a central point called the **integration point** of the system. These points facilitate our connection and interaction with each system, as a point of contact for the fingers or, once you have a little more experience, as a shortcut to connect with the awareness of the respective system quickly.

Often when we've applied an exercise or breathwork for each system individually, at the end we do a final repeat for the entire body, which we call the **megasystem** here. The integration point for the megasystem is on the belly button.

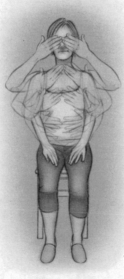

The Hand Positions of Sophrology:
on the Integration Points and Resting

Systems and Integration Points

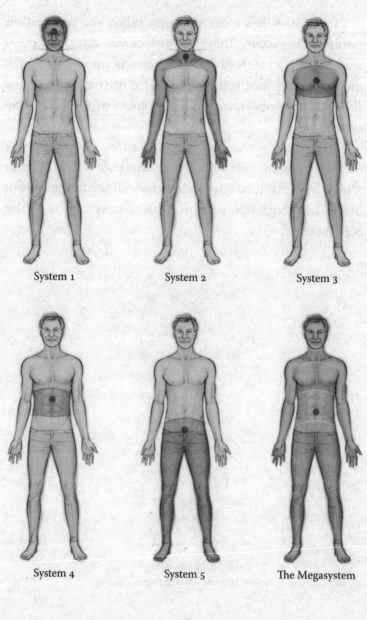

System 1

System 2

System 3

System 4

System 5

The Megasystem

Using The 5 Systems becomes an intuitive connection with the presence of your body, so that in daily life, when stress builds up or when you need to connect with greater confidence before giving a speech, for instance, everything is there to support you through the awareness of your body.

The Postures

Caycedo devised simple sitting and standing postures in which Sophrology is performed to influence the level and state of awareness corresponding to the different phases of the practice – for reaching the sophroliminal state, for letting go of tension or engaging with body awareness. Within one session we often alternate positions.

Remember that Sophrology is also about adaptability, so sometimes a posture is chosen by a practitioner in order to accommodate a particular physical disability or incapacity of the recipient. Those who are highly anxious, angry or exhausted can sometimes find it hard to stay still in a seated position; they may be more suited to processing their tensions through standing movement first. Using a more tailored way to reach a state of stillness ensures that they are more likely to discover that they can achieve a state of relaxation.

These basic postures mirror the movements of everyday life. Again, Sophrology is a practice that fits with life and can be performed with ease on the train, at your desk or at home. In most of the exercises, the eyes are closed as we practise.

The Sitting Relaxed Posture,
also known as The Integration Posture

Sitting Relaxed Posture

You are seated in an upright chair, sitting back relaxed without slumping. You place your hands palm-down on your thighs with your head held straight in the natural alignment of your spine without tension. The hips and knees are at 90 degrees and feet are flat on the floor so that you can feel grounded.

This is the position in which you begin a number of Sophrology practices, and is also used in between activations when you pause to observe your sensation, supporting you to be present and relaxed in the process.

The Pharaoh Posture,
also known as The Activation Posture

Pharaoh Posture

You are again sitting in an upright chair, but this time with your back upright and without leaning back against the chair – a more engaged posture. You can also sit at the front of the chair, so your back is away from the back of the chair. Again, your hips and knee joints should be at 90 degrees and your hands resting on your upper thighs. The shoulders are open and the chin is slightly tucked in. This posture should feel comfortable, with the pelvis in alignment with the rest of the body and nothing forced.

A less relaxed posture, we use this when the practice's intention is to 'activate' our consciousness, allowing us to naturally engage our focus and our awareness using our breath, a simple movement with the arms or to use our voice to make a sound.

The Relaxed Standing Posture

Relaxed Standing Posture

The third basic posture is a standing position. You are standing tall with your feet at shoulder width apart with your head in alignment with your body. This is relaxed standing – you may want to open your shoulders a little to allow freer breathing, or flex your knees slightly if it's more comfy for your back. Your arms and hands are naturally hanging and you are aware of the verticality of your body as your feet connect to the earth.

This is a posture that can also be used to reach the sophroliminal state. Some people prefer it to the sitting relaxed posture, as they might otherwise fall asleep too easily. It is also the posture in which all the exercises of Level 1 are generally performed.

Being Comfortable

Being able to stand for a while feeling comfortable and relaxed seems obvious for someone who is healthy and full of energy. For others it can be hard to achieve, and the Sophrology standing posture or sitting with the back straight can be a posture that needs to be slowly conquered. As you use them a few minutes per day, they will get easier and your energy levels will strengthen too. Gently persevere, always adapting the practice to what feels comfortable and respectful to your state.

'I think what I learnt in that first session was how to relax properly – how to tune out the outside and start focusing inwards on what was in myself. It felt really important to have that moment to tune out all you can hear in your mind and all the noise outside.' Beatrice

Let's Practise

The Foundation Practice consists of three main key techniques or exercises, which together allow you to tune into your sensations and facilitate a powerful change of consciousness and perception. These simple exercises are:

1. **The Body Scan** to relax into the sophroliminal state.
2. Followed by an **activation stretch.**
3. **The Clearing Breath** to acknowledge and clear tensions.
4. Followed by an **integration pause.**
5. **Tune into Your Vital Power** to connect with the power of your consciousness.

Your Guided Practice

The Foundation Practice is recorded as a short 10-minute practice for each of the three key techniques, then a 10-minute practice for the Foundation Practice altogether once you have practised the elements separately. Be guided through the separate key technique exercises several times and get to know them before moving on to the combined practice. This will make all the Sophrology exercises more effective and easier to follow.

The Phenodescription

At the end of every Sophrology session, take a few moments to record your 'phenodescription' – the written record of the sensations that you felt and what your experience was like (your vivance). Although you are being completely non-judgemental about what you experience, you will often feel that there is something different in the body or the mind at the end of the practice. It can be heat, a sense of clarity, or it can be a system or a muscle feeling different from another.

It's like a quick snapshot of experience and thoughts during and after the practice.

This doesn't need to be a long process – if you don't have time, just choose one word that you think best describes the sensations or experience and write it on your smartphone.

As you will start to see, Sophrology has a progression in the way it is practised. This allows body and mind to settle more and more as you develop your awareness and practice, so you can connect more deeply as you let go of unnecessary tensions.

The phenodescription is a simple factual description of what you feel along the way. You may have realised that you started with a very agitated mind, and that going through specific exercises allowed you to let go and tune into a more balanced state. Repetition of the practice is the key to noticing patterns and positive change in your body and mind, and helping you to understand how Sophrology works for you.

A sample phenodescription might read: 'Relaxing. Feel tension in my neck. My eyes move. Breathing more open during the Clearing Breath. Afterwards, feel more energised.' Or simply: 'More energised.'

The 'Tratac'

Before we start any Sophrology practice, I always invite my students to try this super-simple but incredibly powerful 'gesture'. The tratac is an old Sophrology exercise (though no longer taught within Caycedian Sophrology) that I learnt with Gill, my first Sophrologist. I value it and use it with all my clients as it makes everything following more powerful. It helps to engage and calm the mind, increases our power of focus, balances the activity of the brain and helps us tune into the mind–body connection. All within about 15 seconds.

Sit on an upright chair in the sitting relaxed posture, with your eyes open.

Raise one of your arms straight out in front of you so that your hand is clenched with your thumb up. Your arm is slightly higher than eye level so that your thumb is level with your forehead.

Find a mark or a dot on your thumb or thumbnail on which to focus your gaze. Now, inhale and hold your breath, and at the same time bring the thumb slowly towards the place between your eyebrows, keeping both eyes carefully fixed on the 'spot' (so that your eyes 'cross').

When your thumb meets your forehead, immediately close your eyes and exhale, bringing your arms back to lie on your thighs. Repeat if you wish.

Various schools of Zen, yoga and Buddhism are the source of this exercise to align the eye movements with the brain – as vision connects with our mental and emotional state, so we reduce eye movements in order to help bring stillness and presence to our mind. Also, research has shown that a simple tracking-an-object exercise like this causes increased interaction between the right and left hemispheres of the brain to improve performance and boost creativity.

My clients love this exercise. Try it before an important meeting so you can remain focused or, if you are around children, teach them to do this too as they find it really fun to cross the eyes in such a way!

Key Technique 1: The Body Scan 🔊

Now we move on to the key techniques. The **body scan** is the 'door' through which we enter the state of dynamic relaxation. Its aim is to reach a state of 'relaxed alert', or the sophroliminal state, in which transformation is facilitated or made more powerful. The body scan invites the mind to connect with the entire body through the 5 Systems and to relax, so that you are present and able to tune into your physical sensations, emotions and perceptions.

The most important thing to remember about the body scan, and the whole practice of Sophrology, is that there is nothing to achieve, no right or wrong sensation to feel. Maybe you won't even feel anything to start with. Observing and feeling sensation in your body can be difficult, as can fully relaxing. Letting go of what we should feel, visualise or succeed in during the practice is important. Welcome to the worlds of non-judgement and self-acceptance!

Posture: Sitting relaxed, eyes closed. (Don't think you have to stay totally still as a statue! If you need to scratch or

move your shoulders then do it – listen to what your body says.)
Time: 10 minutes

1. Sit in an upright chair with back relaxed, feet placed firmly on the ground with knees at right angles.

2. In that initial position, close your eyes and take a moment to start to feel the presence of your body. Notice your breath as you breathe in and out steadily and deeply. Take a moment to observe the movement of the tummy – with the inhalation the tummy goes out, with the exhalation the tummy goes back to its initial position. (Remember – if your breath doesn't follow that pattern, don't worry, just acknowledge. Things will naturally evolve with the practice.)

3. Once you are ready to start the body scan, bring your attention to the first body system – the head and face. Focus on the presence of the forehead and invite it to relax, then tune into the presence of the eyes – the back of the eyes and the eyelids. Now notice the presence of your cheeks, nose and jaw, allowing your jaw to fully relax. Imagine the brain as a muscle and every time you breathe out it is able to relax more. Feel the presence of the face and head and fully connect with the first system as it relaxes.

4. Now bring your attention to the second system – the presence of the neck and shoulders. Feel the presence of the throat as well, the thyroid gland at the front of

the throat, then moving on to focus on the form of the shoulders, the arms, hands and fingers. Focus your attention on the entire second system, feeling its presence as you breathe and relax.

5. Now move to the third system, focusing your attention on the chest, and allowing the chest area to open and to relax. Feel the presence of the upper back and the shoulder blades, and allow all the muscles of the upper back to relax. Imagine the heart and the lungs inside the chest, sensing the presence of the organs inside the chest and allowing them to relax fully. Tune into the presence of the entire chest, its inner and outer space as they relax.

6. When you are ready, move your attention to the presence of the fourth system. Feel the upper tummy area and the corresponding region of the lower back, helping all the organs of your tummy to relax. Feel or picture the liver on your right, the stomach in the centre and the kidneys round the back and all the digestive organs as they start to ease and relax. Take a moment again to notice the presence of your breath in the fourth system as you breathe in and out. Be aware of the presence of your whole spine and back as they ease.

7. Next, move your attention to your fifth system: the lower tummy, the pelvis, the legs and feet. Be aware of the internal organs in your lower tummy area too and tune into the presence of your pelvic area. Feel the

presence of your thighs, knees, legs and feet, even your toes. Allow your lower back and body area to relax fully. Notice the connection of your feet to the ground.

8. Now, breathe carefully and slowly, feeling the presence of your entire body, grounded on the chair and floor, being fully relaxed. Take a moment to notice all the sensations in your systems and observe the rhythmic movement of your breath.

At the end of the body scan, notice how your body feels, so you can write up your phenodescription later. I advise you to practise this exercise with the recording at least three times before going on to the next. But you can do it as many times as you want, of course!

You may have reached a state where your body feels relaxed and your mind alert. Remember that there is nothing to achieve in Sophrology, though, so if this exercise was a challenge for you, or if you found it hard to focus, just notice that. The next part of the introductory exercises will help you find more serenity as you release the tensions that your connected body can possibly now sense.

Activation Stretch

Now, briefly before you release the tensions from your body and deepen the connection between the mind and body, we do a quick body activation stretch. The aim of this quick movement is to tune deeper into the presence of your body in your consciousness. As we said before, it is so easy to be in the mind most of the time and forget about the sensations our body gives us.

Keeping your eyes closed, move into the pharaoh posture and connect to the presence of your whole body. Interlace your fingers and turn your hands so your palms face outwards, inhale and bring the arms straight up above your head and hold them there. Hold your breath and lightly tense the entire body, from the head to the feet, to activate the presence of the body in the consciousness.

On the release of breath, bring the arms down as you notice your body sensations.

This stretch is usually done after the body scan and before moving to the clearing breath. You can also use it throughout your day, when you notice that you are too much in your head or when your body feels tense sitting at your computer. It is a way to quickly ground in your body and let go of tensions.

Key Technique 2: The Clearing Breath 🔊

Our next technique, the clearing breath, allows us to feel and acknowledge any unnecessary tensions and stresses within the body and let them go through the power of the out breath. As you breathe out, you can emphasise the breath by using sound to 'push' out the breath and tension, with a 'huff' if this feels right. Try also to lengthen your out breath as it will help you relax more.

Initially we concentrate more on physical tension as a manifestation of all other tensions, as it's probably easier to feel, but as you close your eyes you may sense tension in the mind as well. Maybe your chest is very tight or your head is full of stuff – negative thoughts and emotions? You may find it hard to feel a change in the systems, so it might help to use your imagination with images like a dark plume of smoke that is liberated from the integration point, or another image that helps you to connect with that sensation of letting go. I usually advise using up to three breaths on each system, but when you are more experienced and able to feel what works for you, you may feel that one out breath per system is enough to clear it, or decide to stay longer on a system that manifests more tensions. In traditional Sophrology, we call this exercise the 'release of negative tension', but I prefer to remove the negative aspect as tension can serve a purpose and also represents the link between the mind and body, so I focus on tension in all forms as we work to acknowledge and then release through the breath. Working from the sophroliminal state and supported by the power of the breath, this simple practice brings a major shift in your consciousness.

Breathing Through the Mouth and Nose

I usually invite beginners to inhale through the nose and exhale through the mouth for this exercise as it supports the lengthening of the out breath. If you are more experienced in breathing techniques and used to breathing only through the nose, that is fine. See what works best for you!

Posture: Pharaoh, eyes closed.
Time: 10 minutes

1. Remain in the pharaoh posture from the activation stretch, with your hands resting on your thighs.
2. From the activation posture, reach up and position the tips of the fingers of both hands on the integration point of the first system, a point in between your eyebrows, so you are now connected with the first system. Through the touch we connect to that first system, feeling the sensation and noticing any tension in the head and face. Then we just inhale, focusing on the tensions of the first system and, on the exhale, using our intention, we imagine breathing out the tension. Repeat twice more.
   Then go to the second system. Place the fingertips on the integration point for the second system – the thyroid gland at the centre of the throat – keeping

your elbows down and relaxed. Feel any and all of the tension of the second system – inhaling – and let it go with the out breath. Repeat twice or until you feel the tension released.

3. Repeat with the third system, the chest and upper back, placing the fingertips of both hands on the integration point at the centre of the breastbone to connect with the chest. Use the breath to release the tension. Repeat twice more.

4. Then touch the fourth system's integration point at the centre of the upper tummy area just below the ribcage, and use the exhalation to release tension in the tummy, the key organs and the back. Repeat twice more.

5. Then to the fifth system; place your fingers on the integration point below the belly button and above the pubic bone. Take a moment to feel any tension, then breathe out the tension of the lower body. And again, repeat twice more.

6. Finish on the belly button, which connects you with your megasystem and therefore your entire body, and breathe out any remaining tension.

7. Then sit back and take your integration pause before going into the next exercise.

Integration Pause

As I mentioned earlier, alternating movement and stillness is crucial to Sophrology. We activate, and then we 'listen'.

After the Clearing Breath, you take a pause – known as an integration pause – observing the sensations in your systems following the activation you have just practised. It is a pause to do nothing, to just be and notice. It allows the effects of the practice to 'integrate' or settle onto the body and mind, as in the snowstorm toy analogy on page 67. We now wait quietly for the sensation – the 'snow' – to fall and settle, and for our body, mind and spirit to find its new position.

It might seem strange but we require focus to pause properly, to fully relax into the body so that our body can absorb its change, and to remember that we're not trying to reach or to do anything during this time. Simply sit relaxed in the chair with your eyes closed and feel the presence of each system in the body. It can be done quickly or slowly, as you naturally feel. Listen for sensation or prompts from the body, without this being the aim.

Again, listen to your sensation after this exercise. Try to practise the Clearing Breath three or four times over the next few days so that you become used to how it feels.

Key Technique 3: Tune into Your Vital Power ◁))

Now that you have taken the time to integrate following your Clearing Breath, we reach the final part of the Foundation Practice. We are going to tune into the body and look for pleasant sensations. What can you feel in your 5 Systems following the breathwork and clearing you have just done? Common sensations could be: lightness, heat, warmth, heaviness, tingling or space. Do you feel a system that is perhaps more relaxed than others, or a different sense of flow in some part of your body?

These sensations are telling you that your body is alive, constantly adjusting its physiology to serve you. By focusing on these sensations, we are also engaging with the vital power, the source of our inner resources and our balance. This is a perfect example of the positive somatisation I was telling you about earlier on page 60. Here you are connecting with the living potential of your body and consciousness. Over time, noticing the presence of your body through these pleasant sensations will reset the connection you have with your body. You won't only be drawn to the tension your body manifests but also to all the positive messages. We often refer to our body as if it is something that is separate from our own self. With this exercise we are starting to be more unified: body, mind and soul.

Posture: Sitting relaxed, eyes closed.
Time: 10 minutes

1. Sit back in your seat again, hands placed on the top of your legs, in the sitting relaxed posture. Breathe calmly and evenly.
2. Firstly, inhale and stimulate your vital power into your first system. Tune into your sensation and notice what feels pleasant and alive in your systems.

3. As you inhale, use your intention and concentration to stimulate the positive energy of your vital power.

4. As you exhale, imagine that you are sending your vital power around your first system. Imagine the energy pushing into the skin of your first system, into the muscles, bones and into your brain. And repeat.

5. Now tune into and inhale your vital power into your second system – and then use your mind to push the positive energy around the second system, feeling the energy like a light shining through your body and spreading warmth and energy. And repeat for this system.

6. Then repeat twice with the third, fourth and fifth systems, inhaling the positive energy and defusing it throughout the systems with the exhale.

7. And then inhale and exhale your vital power into your whole body, your muscles, your skin, your organs and bones. This energy is flowing through your entire consciousness. Feel it in the way your feet touch the ground and as your body holds you upright.

8. Finish slowly. Take the time to return gently from the sophroliminal state, keeping all this positive energy with you for the next part of your day.

This simple and effective exercise provides a unique space for your body to take on board your message of positivity. You are invited to be deeply in the moment. Just listen and observe your sensations as you inhale and exhale. You may be conscious of a particular part of your system, a muscle that feels tighter or an organ that you want to target in particular, to bring more vital power into it. Or you may find it difficult to feel anything yet – if so, don't worry.

A Happy Word or Image

One way of activating your positive inner resources is to choose or create your own personal happy image while in the sophroliminal state or to find an inspiring word to use with the practice. For the image, it should represent a place where you feel at ease, happy, relaxed and calm, or a place where you feel it is easy to replenish your energy or recuperate. It is usually a place in nature. Maybe a recent place you have visited during a holiday where you noticed beauty and space, or a childhood landscape where you have good memories, or simply a creation of the perfect natural environment where you can include as many wonders of nature as you like: water elements (waterfalls, a lake, the sea), trees and flowers, mountains or desert. Once you have managed to visualise your happy place, imagine how it would feel if you were there, exploring this space with your senses. Can you add an appealing scent, of your favourite flower or your favourite dish? Do you note some attractive colours? Can you feel a warm breeze on your skin or the comforting gentle heat of the sun?

Note the effects this has on your body and your systems and use the breath to stimulate these pleasant sensations in the body in the same way you did earlier with your vital power. If visualisation is not your thing, just let a positive word come to mind, something like calm, confidence, joy, etc. Synchronise that word with your in breath and out breath as a way to tune into its benefits.

The word or your landscape will become more and more precise and a very easy way to access positivity, calm and relaxation, for this is what you find in it. You will simply need to close your eyes, connect with one of them and your brain will immediately connect you with empowering sensations.

A Daily Habit

I am often asked where and when Sophrology should be practised. Ideally, just find a chair you can comfortably sit in and a space where you have some quiet for 10 minutes. But if you only have a sofa and a noisy family around you, don't let it stop you! Secure the space so everybody is safe, plug in your headset and start. If the only 10 minutes you can find are during your commute to work – then start there and over time I hope Sophrology will help you to find 10 minutes somewhere else in your day.

There is no right time of the day to perform these exercises – find a space in your day that works for you. Before bed can be good – it will help you to relax. If you are highly stressed and find it hard to focus, you may find that during your first week of practice you struggle to concentrate and follow the practice. If you fall asleep, then you're really exhausted! Tell yourself that you are doing great. This Foundation Practice is the first step to knowing yourself, your mind and body, better. Your body is telling you what it needs. If you are agitated and find it hard to sit still, think: 'Thank you very much for telling me, body'. You are clearly in overdrive. Look after yourself and just acknowledge your state without judgement as much as you can and carry on creating this time each day for yourself.

You are now learning the parts of the Foundation Practice and experiencing your first sensations with Sophrology. If you listen to the recordings a few times, the unfolding of these steps will become easier for you as both mind and body will have 'recorded' them. You will then be able to concentrate on your sensation or vivance rather than where to focus, the position of the systems, or when to do the integration pause. Before each session, remember to avoid any preconceived idea of what you might experience in terms of sensations, as your vivance will constantly evolve from one day to the next. That is why each time it is a new experience to add to your library of sensations, perceptions, images or feelings. This is the way consciousness is 'unveiled'. Over a short period of time, things will start to shift and change, you will feel more energised and a greater clarity and efficiency will soon appear in what you pursue.

The Foundation Practice and the Level 1 exercises in the next section are about further balancing the body and mind but also they increase energy levels, so if you are a light sleeper you might want to do those in the morning rather than just before bed. (Over time, they will also help you sleep better too.) All the other practices can be done anywhere at any time, sitting or standing, and they are also great done just before sleep to let go of the tension of your day and prepare for a good night's sleep.

The Foundation Practice 🔊
Time: 10 minutes

Remember to practise each of these three techniques separately three or four times first, then you will be ready to do the key techniques in one go over a shorter time, in the one 10-minute recording. We can move slightly faster once you are familiar with where your systems are, and with the exercises and their primary intention.

The unique nature of Sophrology is to be able to quickly tune in and be efficient about the way we connect with ourselves. As we progress through Level 1 and then the supertools, your Foundation Practice can become shorter. It will be part of your body memory and you will be able to use it 'on the go' too, extracting what you find most efficient from it. A few clearing out breaths when you feel anxiety kicking in on the way to meet someone, a quick body scan when you need to ground if feeling overactive and unable to focus, or simply inhaling beauty and vitality and bringing it into your systems during a walk in the woods. This will become a part of you and will be such a helpful life skill to have.

Foundation Practice 'On the Go'

The fantastic thing about Sophrology is that it's completely portable – and created to be used during the day when you need an instant hit of serenity, confidence or de-stressing. Whether you are on the move, need to perform your Foundation Practice quickly or are having a Sophrology 'top-up' during a tough or tiring day, here's a way to squeeze in the complete Foundation Practice in about 2 minutes using the power of the integration points of the systems (this exercise was devised by Claudia Sanchez and Ricardo Lopez – see page 223).

As with all Sophrology, this quick-fix version will only be effective when you have practised the full-length Foundation Practice several times first to help your mind and body learn the correct 'route' to this level of connection and relaxation.

1. You are standing with eyes open. Take one or two deep breaths to consciously connect with the breath and the presence of the body.
2. Now, for the Clearing Breath, simply bring your

clenched fists together in front of your forehead – the integration point of the first system. Inhale, bring a light tension to the fist and first system as you connect with possible tensions in the region, then exhale all of the tensions. As you exhale, let your arms fall to your side, symbolically releasing all the tensions of the system.

3. Repeat with fists in front of the integration points for the second, third, fourth and fifth systems, exhaling the tensions as your arms fall to your side.

4. Finish with your fists in front of the belly button for the megasystem. Then pause and just notice the sensation for a moment.

5. Now, breathing calmly and with knees slightly bent, hold your arms curved out in front of you – as if you are holding something large and round.

6. With a positive intention in mind (such as a word like calm, joy, confidence), now raise your arms slowly above the head, inhaling and tuning into your chosen positive.

7. Then, exhale through the mouth, bringing the hands slowly back down, palms facing downwards now as if gently pushing something back down, infusing your body with the positive intention as you do so.

8. Now that you have completed the quick version of the Foundation Practice, take a few moments to pause and listen for sensation.

The Foundation Practice – Summary

- We view the body as 5 Systems for the purposes of the Sophrology exercises and connecting with consciousness.
- The Foundation Practice is formed of the three key techniques that begin every full Sophrology session:
  - The Body Scan
  - The Clearing Breath
  - Tune into Your Vital Power.
- The Foundation Practice is the beginning of all Sophrology practices and is a set of exercises that will help with stress, sleep problems and confidence.

CASE STUDY: **PAOLA** – 'SO MUCH MORE CONFIDENT IN MY ABILITIES.'

Paola is a massage therapist and part-time writer who was looking for help to deal with the overwhelming stress of everyday life and lack of self-confidence, plus support to transition to a full-time writing career.

I had tried many meditation and mindfulness techniques, and as a body therapist was reasonably aware of my body, so Sophrology felt very natural when I started. I thought that it worked really fast in terms of me feeling the beneficial effects straight away. I'm very fidgety so it can be a struggle to get the right amount of concentration to focus on breathing – I find meditation quite frustrating in that way. As you're going through a sequence of exercises, your rational mind doesn't have the time to take over so by the time I have focused on the breathing, moving the muscles and maybe visualising something I don't have the mental space for anything else. Which is good if you're prone to worry like myself. If you have something better to replace those thoughts and worries, everything starts to feel lighter.

I think my own starting point is probably different from the average person. When you're a body therapist, your level of body awareness tends to be higher. But I think even if you're not a therapist and you start from scratch with Sophrology, you start identifying patterns about what your body is saying. And sometimes you get a headache or back pain – you think, 'I'll just work through it, I'll be fine.' But if you take the time to understand your body better you may pick up on things before they become chronic. You might be able to stop things in their track before they get worse.

When it comes to making big changes in my life, like many people I can be defeatist. Sometimes I don't even try something because I think I'm going to fail. When you're lacking confidence, you think, 'What's the point in trying, I'm not going to make it. I'm not going to do it.' Working on my self-development, finding my inner strength has made me more capable of achieving things I didn't think possible before. I'm in the process of moving countries and I know that if I just allowed the old me to take over, I wouldn't even entertain the thought. Sophrology has made me feel so much more confident in my abilities. In terms of my writing work, now when I pitch for a project, I seem to have found the magic formula to be accepted. I think when you believe in yourself you're more likely to be able to convince a potential client that they should hire you. Also, I find that if I take the time to do the relaxation before I write, the actual quality of my writing will improve. I think I do my best writing when I'm in the relaxed state of mind.

When I do practise in my day-to-day life, it's because I need to make sense of what is happening to me. When life is hectic and you're chasing your tail, you forget what is a priority and what isn't. You get used to being busy for the sake of it and sometimes you have to let go of activities that are not productive. If we don't make enough time to embrace some form of relaxation, we might feel completely overwhelmed.

15 Minutes to Balance Your Body and Mind: The Level 1 Practice

You might be wondering why you should be spending your time breathing in positivity or tensing your body systems in order to change your life. What difference can activating your body in your consciousness make to your daily life?

The Level 1 practice embodies the core of Sophrology in its focus on the body. Through the alternance of gentle standing movements and sitting pauses, plus the control of the breath, we are able to let go of our tensions and positively ground ourselves in our bodies. Learning to connect more deeply to our system is like connecting the dots between the different parts of our body so we become more unified and aware of the presence of our body.

Level 1 is the level to practise for those whose minds are racing all the time, who are constantly a step ahead in their mind and find it difficult to stay still or rest. It will work wonders on anxiety, and when we feel overwhelmed by life or unable to let go. The body movements and sensations focus the mind, coupled with concentration on breathing, and you will soon find out that you can no longer think about your worries and you will naturally feel more present.

'*It helps me to understand that we can have pressure, we can have stress. But if there's too much I can just take it down to zero and then I can go again.*' Penelope

Level 1 is also a journey through your 5 Systems, giving you a chance to explore them in depth. Through the simple movements and breathing techniques, the exercises are designed to balance the body and mind, allowing us to let go of present and past energy blocks and tensions. The increased oxygenation of the brain and body as the body is gently mobilised will give us more energy if we are exhausted and will ground us and help us to relax if we are agitated and overstimulated. Again, we go back to the concept that our body knows what we need to help and how to heal ourselves, and we have the ability here to connect with that deep knowledge and stimulate the vital energy.

Practised regularly over a month, you can expect it to help you:

- improve your sleep quality
- reduce the tension of your body and mind
- manage stress effectively
- aid recuperation
- restore and balance your energy levels
- lift your mood and increase positivity
- increase your ability to focus
- feel more relaxed in daily life

- diminish anxiety
- have greater clarity
- gain stronger focus on your goals
- feel more confident and hopeful
- be more emotionally stable
- feel more grounded
- be more present and live in the here and now

That's rather impressive, isn't it!

The path of Sophrology is full of surprises as we connect to our true potentials. I often have clients who will come for a specific issue and realise that by working on it, their overall experience of life shifts, helping them to support other aspects of their daily lives. Being able to connect to your superpower really makes the difference and will take you where you are ready to go; it's a real and positive adventure you are going into as you practise.

So that you can get a taste of what Level 1 is and start to enjoy its benefit, I have selected some of its exercises and created two practices with them. In the purest Sophrology form, there are notably more exercises for each system and we usually sit down between each system's activation for the integration pause – something I encourage you to experience once you know the exercises well.

The Level 1 practice here consists of a quick Foundation Practice first, followed by a specific exercise for each of the 5 Systems, performed standing. I have divided the practice into two 15-minute sections so that it can be practised as a full 30-minute or as a shorter 15-minute session, depending on what you feel you need and how much time and head-space you have available.

Level 1 – Part 1 🔊

Posture: Relaxed standing, eyes closed.
Time taken: 15 minutes

Tratac
Simple Foundation Practice Standing
Tune in 1: Head Rotation
Tune in 2: Shoulder Pump
Tune in 3: The Windmill
Integration pause

We start with our simple short Foundation Practice – the key techniques – (guided with my voice) but this time standing, followed by three simple exercises designed to engage specifically with the first three systems of the body, and therefore more deeply with our consciousness.

Let's get started and, as with all Sophrology, don't worry about the precision of the movements or breathing – the most important thing to bring is awareness and intention to your practice. This is all you need. There is no right or wrong way to practise, no one thing that you must achieve – just enjoy the practice and feel present to the sensations that occur without judgement on what it is or what you should feel. Go into each practice with an open mind and see what manifests.

Tune into the First System: Head Rotation

System 1: Head Rotation

Following the audio, you will start with a tratac and short standing Foundation Practice. I recommend performing this practice with a chair behind you in case you need to rest during the exercises.

1. As you stand comfortably, inhaling and exhaling, connect with the presence of your first system of your body – your head and face.

2. First exhale through your mouth, then inhale through the nose, hold your breath, then move the head slowly about 90 degrees to face to your right, then over to look to the left, then back to the centre. Remember to respect the limits of your body; it is not about exercising but rather the awareness and sensation of the movement.

3. Once you feel you need to breathe out, just bring the head back in line with the body and exhale through the mouth. Take a moment to notice your sensations in the first system as you allow it to fully relax. (You may feel slightly light-headed due to your large intake of oxygen. Just make sure you are standing in front of your chair so that you can choose to sit down and give time to your sensation to settle again if you need to.)

4. Continue and repeat the move once more. Then bring the head back to the centre and exhale. You can do this move quite swiftly.

5. Observe the sensation briefly in the first system before the next movement.

Tune into the Second System: Shoulder Pump

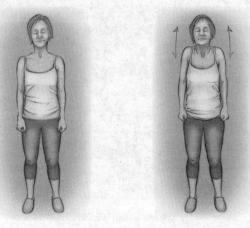

System 2: Shoulder Pump

Now we focus on the presence of the second system – the neck, throat, shoulders, arms and hands.

Clench your hands into fists at your side. Exhale with your mouth and inhale with your nose, then hold the breath and 'pump' your shoulders up and down for several seconds. (The pumping move takes your shoulders up towards your ears at the same time and then back down again with the arms held straight.) Then exhale while you open your hands and relax your arms again.

Listen briefly for sensation. Then repeat once more. Now take a few moments to listen for sensation in the system before the next exercise.

Tune into the Third System: The Windmill

System 3: The Windmill

1. Stand comfortably, and exhale through your mouth. Inhale and bring your hands up and rest your fingertips on each shoulder.

2. Hold your breath. Now, with elbows pointing out to the side, rotate your arms so that your elbows reach up towards your ears, and down against your body. Do several rotations.

3. Then exhale and release your arms. Take a pause to listen to the sensation in your chest and upper back. Repeat the move.

4. Finish with an integration pause sitting, noticing your sensation in the systems that you have now activated, and take a moment to tune into the vital power of your first three systems.

5. This is an excellent time to tune into any positive sensations or thoughts that can help you on your path. Are you looking for confidence? Then inhale confidence on the in breath, and on the out breath diffuse it into your first three systems. It could also be calm, joy, relaxation, tranquillity, positive energy or healing.

At the end of this section, you can either carry on and complete the second part or, if you wish to finish, make your slow return and enjoy your phenodescription.

Adapting Level 1 to Your Needs

Level 1 practice is partly performed standing, therefore it can be challenging for those who perhaps lack energy or have pain. Remember that the practice of Sophrology is adaptable and should meet you where you are, so work out how you can make it work for you. You might choose to concentrate on one system and then sit to recuperate. Over time it will help your energy levels to increase. You may choose to do these exercises sitting, and simply adapt them so you can still enjoy their benefits and observe the sensations they generate. The whole point of Sophrology is to tune in and find what works for you. Never force a position or a move. It is not about doing gymnastics or building muscle power, it is about being mindful of what is happening as you perform the motions and then pause. Do these exercises gently or more energetically depending your level of fitness and what you like or need in the moment.

Level 1 – Part 2 🔊

Posture: Standing relaxed, eyes closed.
Time taken: 15 minutes
Tratac
Simple Foundation Practice Standing

Tune in 4: The Bellows
Tune in 5: Walking
Tune into the Megasystem: Body Halves
Integration pause

For the second part of this practice, the exercises can be directly added to the first to give you a complete Level 1 practice, or use this as its own Sophrology session, starting with the tratac and short Foundation Practice standing. Take your time to reach that stage; there is no advantage in rushing the practice. Going into the depth of the method requires repetition and, as we have said before, a shorter but more frequent practice is better than a one-hour-long practice once in a while.

Tune into the Fourth System: The Bellows

The Bellows

1. Begin with the tratac and short standing Foundation Practice.

2. Now, stand comfortably, inhaling and exhaling, and connect with the presence of your fourth system. Place one hand on your tummy and the other hand on your lower back.

3. Now inhale through the nose and 'huff' the breath out – forcing it out of the nose with a sound and feeling the movement of the tummy with your hand. Concentrate on contracting and bringing your tummy in as you push the air out through your nose. Then release the tummy and your in breath will naturally follow. Repeat it. You may want to start slowly and then gently increase the speed of the breath and contraction of your tummy until the whole things sounds like a steam train!

4. Then pause, listen and do the exercise once more. You can breathe in and out quickly or slowly depending on your state of mind and whether the action feels more therapeutic completed swiftly. End with a few moments of pause while you listen for sensation.

Note: Caution for Pregnant Women

I don't recommend this exercise for pregnant women as they may find their tummy more tense afterwards. Generally, Level 1 is suitable for pregnancy but I advise you to leave the breath component out as it may be too stimulating. It all depends what you are used to doing in your daily life or exercise, of course.

Tune into the Fifth System: Walking

System 5: Walking

Stand comfortably relaxed, breathing easily and feeling both feet in connection with the floor. Tune into the presence of your fifth system: namely the pelvis, the lower abdominal organs, the pelvic floor, legs and feet.

Keeping your breathing normal, start 'walking' on the spot, lifting the back of one foot at a time (but keeping the toes connected to the ground). You can go faster if you have more energy. Listen to your sensations.

Do this for approximately 20 seconds then pause, listen and repeat once more. Again, take a moment to pause and listen for sensation.

Tune in Together: Body Halves (The Megasystem)

Megasystem: Body Halves

Stand comfortably relaxed, breathing deeply and tuning into the presence of your entire body, all your systems in one. Now move your weight to your right leg, inhale, clench your right fist and reach your right arm straight up in the air. Tense the entire right side of your body, from your clenched fist down to your right foot, and then exhale, bringing your right arm to your side. Bring your body weight back to the centre and take a moment to notice your sensation. Note the difference between the left and right sides of the body.

Now, move your body weight onto your left foot, inhale and tense the left side of the body and reach above your head. Exhale and release the tension, and bring your arm down. Notice the sensation.

Then stand firmly with your weight spread equally on both feet and do the exercise with both sides of the body together – inhale, tense and reach up. Then exhale and release. Repeat again.

Then sit down and complete the Level 1 practice with a final integration pause or the object visualisation that you find below.

Do your slow return (see below) and your phenodescription.

Returning from the Sophroliminal State

As you have now noticed, it takes a little while to reach the sophroliminal state and it can also take a few moments to gently come out of it. Like when you wake up in the morning, don't rush it. You might want to start by wiggling a toe or moving your hands as you remember where you are and feel the presence of your body starting to move and adapt to a more alert state of consciousness. You could fully stretch or rub your hands together or stroke different parts of body or face to help you come back to your usual state of awareness. If you were very relaxed and went very far, it may take a few minutes until you are ready to talk and get on with your daily activities. So allow this time before you sit in your car or go out in the world. You can feel a bit spaced out!

And don't forget to notice, or preferably write down, your phenodescription. You may note that some systems are easier to feel than others initially, and that some days you can go deeper than others.

What if Level 1 Generates Tensions or Resistance?

When we finally relax and connect, these tensions emerge in our consciousness and we feel them. What should we do? Simply keep the practice going and ensure you do a good Foundation Practice beforehand. Those tensions should dissipate as you build up your inner resources. If they persist, it is a good idea to complement your Sophrology practice with manual therapy such as osteopathy, massage, shiatsu or acupuncture, which will help speed up the process of release.

Object Visualisation

In the traditional Sophrology approach, Level 1 finishes with an object visualisation exercise.

Once you are seated in your integration pause after the standing work, you have finished the stimulation of the positives in your body. Simply invite onto your inner screen the image of an object of daily life – something very standard and nothing you associate with emotion, such as a glass, a fork or a flower. The aim of this exercise is to train your ability to visualise and to concentrate. It also helps focus the mind further and stop it wandering. As you view the object, create its shape and change its colour and size. You might play with these components once you have managed to make your picture. You can also do this exercise without any preparation while sitting on the bus if you are struggling with negative thoughts.

Over time and through repetition, the practice of Level 1 Sophrology establishes a deeper connection and awareness of the sensation in our body, enabling us to grow in confidence and to recentre ourself when life gets in the way.

By using the 5 Systems, we are bringing our attention into each region so that each area becomes more present in our consciousness. As a result, our relationship with each system of our body starts to shift and we are more able to notice and let go of tension, whether conscious or unconscious. We are supporting our body to bring us back into balance as well as growing in awareness.

Don't underestimate the benefits of Level 1 even if you are already an experienced Sophrology lover! After 20 years of practice I regularly go back to it in my daily life. A simple shoulder pump or grounding yourself through walking on the spot can transform the rest of your day. The immediate clarity it gives through your increased connection to your body and the increased oxygenation has often saved an afternoon of work after a late night, or allowed me to gather my thoughts after seeing a client and before the next. Some people will just take Level 1 from Sophrology and never go beyond that if they are purely looking into the stress-management benefits of Sophrology. It is a tool for life and, if you do nothing else, then performing this set of exercises every day for a fortnight would see a huge shift in your approach to life. The transformation you get from practising it for a while will give you a true understanding of what I mean by being able to tune into consciousness and its vital power as well as be more in the present moment. For now, keep repeating this set of exercises to deepen your dynamic relaxation practice and to make Sophrology part of your daily life. As you become used to them, I would expect this practice to take just 6 to 8 minutes of your day – time very well spent!

15 Minutes to Balance your Body and Mind – Summary

- This Level 1 practice embodies the importance of the body and the mind–body connection in Sophrology.
- It is a great practice for those who struggle with anxiety and are overwhelmed by daily life. Practise regularly to see a significant improvement in emotional resilience, stress relief and sleep quality.
- This practice also allows you to explore your 5 Systems in more depth, enhancing your relationship with your body.

Benjamin, 18, is a professional tennis player, and sought out Sophrology to help him with performance anxiety and to increase his confidence on the tennis court.

Tennis is such a high-pressure sport. I suffer with self-confidence, which is really frustrating. I have a busy schedule – training about five hours a day plus fitness work plus travelling to where I train, so it's really demanding. And I found that when I was playing I couldn't get the most out of it because of my confidence issues.

Dominique helped me come to the root of why I was feeling like that. She gave me some recordings. I liked it because it went straight to the issue and you can adapt it to when and wherever you need it. She gave me this exercise where you clench your hand really deeply and then release (The Reflex, page 160). And it's such a simple exercise but it went a really long way for me. I just clench my toes – you can adapt it so this way I can do it during a match without it being obvious to those watching. I use it in matches a lot between sets if I'm feeling down or I'm under a lot of pressure. I do the clench and the release and then it's just as if everything goes away, it clears my mind and I feel so much more relaxed. And another exercise that helped was the sleep visualisation – after a long day I'd get home and I'd be really tired but I'd have problems switching off and sleeping. And basically you just think of something or a place that makes you happy (see *The Sleep Gatekeeper*, page 166). I think of a park near my house. And you just 'go' there when you close your eyes – it's like you're there. It's so simple and it's amazing what it can do.

I can't explain how much it's helped. Before I started doing Sophrology, I just felt too much within myself – not just with tennis, but with life. I felt stressed all the time. But when I started using it, even after the first session, my whole outlook changed. I didn't feel that stressed any more. I got a better night's sleep as well. It's as if it's letting go of bad emotions and you can move on. And you don't have to linger on stuff. In the exercises, you feel it, acknowledge it and let it go.

I find it really helpful to do the lying down exercise. I breathe in my intention – my words are confidence and relaxation – you breathe it in and you've let out all the negative emotions. I'm going to use it for a big tournament coming up. Right now I might not be feeling too confident about it but you visualise yourself on the court and how you want your match to be and your play to be, and you visualise *yourself winning and getting the trophy and everything (see Enjoy a Bright Future, page 181). It's kind of like thinking things into existence.*

I used it last year. I was nervous about going to a tennis academy in Spain. From about two months before, I visualised how I wanted my time to be there, and how I wanted to feel and how I wanted to play well. And when I went there I played the best game I'd ever played. It was incredible.

10 Minutes to Change Your Daily Life: The Supertool Practice

We've talked of the gentle superpower of Sophrology, and it is really in the changes it can make to your daily life that Sophrology finds its strengths. What difference would it make to your life if you could find calm whenever you needed, if you could shield yourself from the chaos and stresses around you, and if you could find the positive in whatever the day throws at you? In Sophrology we see these core skills – confidence, harmony, resilience – as abilities that our body instinctively knows and that our consciousness owns and has within, if only we connect more.

Now that you have experienced the Foundation and Level 1 Practice of Sophrology together, I hope you have already noticed changes in your mood, energy or awareness through regular use of the basic practice. Here, I have chosen the tools that I frequently use with beginners as they are simple and powerful – and as part of a simple practice, they take just 12 minutes to fit into your day.

'I used to really worry, over-think and be stressed about exams and work. This could often lead to nausea and an

inability to focus on anything else but the problem or anxiety I was confronted with. With Dominique I learnt to control my nerves and centre myself. Now instead of feeling dizzy from worrying about everything, I feel more whole as a person and far more confident. It really is amazing how Sophrology can change the way you think and feel and encourage you to take a more relaxed approach.' Emily

In order to target your Sophrology practice and to know where to start with the supertools below, just take a moment and choose one situation in your life you struggle with. If there are several, just let one come to mind. All of our resources are all interconnected in consciousness, so by regularly working on one aspect of consciousness, you will naturally strengthen all your other resources.

Ask yourself what would help you to better deal with that person, that situation or worry – I mean in terms of your inner resources, the thing that you can control. Would more calm and focus help you express yourself more clearly to someone? Do you feel so stressed that you are about to burst, or are you angry and thinking that letting go of that feeling could change the game? Are you preparing for an important event and would like to feel fully positive and confident in your capabilities? Are you stuck with negative beliefs about yourself or the world around you that hold you back in your daily life? Do you need to be able to recentre yourself on the spot during a meeting or during events that trigger anxiety? Are your whole life and health disturbed because you simply lack sleep and struggle with your energy?

These are the obvious applications for the supertools I present, but everybody is different, and I invite you to trust which exercise you are drawn to. Taking the time to think about and set your intention ahead of these exercises and choose the theme that resonates most with you will make them far more effective as you are clear and positive about what you want to achieve.

The supertools will help you with:

Calm and Headspace: Clarity (The Bubble, page 135)

Releasing Stress and Anger: Letting Go (The Pump, page 141)

Confidence and Success: Confidence (The Magic Picture, page 149)

Letting Go of Negativity: Positivity (The Bag, page 154)

Instant Calm: Resilience (The Reflex Sign, page 160)

Sleep and Managing Energy: A Calm Sleep Environment (The Sleep Gatekeeper, page 166)

Which of these would transform your life? How would it feel to achieve this goal? Again, think mindfully and with a clear hope about what you want to achieve – the clearer you are in what you want to achieve, the more likely you are to reach that state.

How Do the Practices Work?

The supertools are short exercises designed to bring together our breathing, movement, awareness and intention to produce dynamic connections to effect change. And the exciting news about these supertools is that not only are they simple to remember and hugely effective through regular use, but they are designed so that once we have practised them several times in full and at a time of calm, we will be able to use them in our daily life, out and about, to bring about an instant solution to our problem. We 'train' our supertool in the sophroliminal state so that we are later able to access it 'on the go' whenever we need support. Now, let's get started!

Calm and Headspace

This is a superb practice for when we are feeling agitated, overstimulated, or simply overwhelmed with life. Perhaps you're feeling a little chaotic in your mind – or worrying about everything and losing sight of what is important and what isn't. Hands up then, everyone! It is a very likely state for a lot of us as we can often feel that a lot of demands are put on us. This morning I found myself trying to feed my child and worrying about all the things that I wanted to fit into my schedule that day.

Without being careful, having too much to do becomes the norm. But most important is how we feel about it all. Some people achieve a massive amount of work and go through difficult experiences while staying naturally centred, but for others the slightest change in their plans or excess of demands on them makes them highly anxious. It is our inner state that determines our daily experience of life, how we respond to the life we live, and therefore how stressed we really are. And that is one thing that we can have control over.

Imagine if you could get on with your daily tasks without worry, in a calm state, taking one thing after the other and trusting the present moment? Imagine feeling that everything that is happening has its right place in your day rather than fighting it? When we are calm and clear-headed we lose less time on things that don't matter and we are less likely to get drawn into actions we don't want to do or don't need to do. It allows us to connect with a sense of clarity.

Through this practice, we invite in calm and clarity, and we aim to feel more in control of ourselves and more grounded and connected to our inner self through the bodywork. Quite simply, our brains and our bodies are struggling to cope, and we just need to stop and listen to them, to listen to ourselves!

We talked earlier about the power of 'being', not 'doing' all the time, and this is a huge part of Sophrology. We want to take time out, to stop, and to be present in our true self – THINK LESS, BE MORE.

Inner Resource: Clarity

For me, clarity is to do with our perceptions. When we are calm and grounded, we are more likely to feel clear about ourselves or the world around us, to know what our priorities are, to discern and understand what is happening, and to remain centred and in tune with our needs, desires and inner resources. It is also very useful in setting our goals and being clear about our wishes and intentions for our future.

It is difficult to have clarity in such a busy world, but without learning to listen to ourselves and find our own balance we will struggle to cope with what life throws at us. At the heart of Level 1 and Level 2 Sophrology is the linking of mind and body, using the connection to cut through the noise of everything and everyone around us to allow us to relearn how to truly listen to what our body and mind are telling us, and to give us the power to say 'Stop'. To 'be' rather than to 'do'.

And clarity is also about looking to the future. Perhaps we've forgotten all about our life goals or given up on having a purpose in life? Perhaps we are too busy thinking of all the things that we need to do for others, without taking any time or space for ourselves? Whatever our problems or stresses might be, we need clarity in order to find our focus, and to answer the important questions that guide us to understand our best way to live.

Imagine that, like a superhero, you have a shield with special powers. With that shield, you can protect yourself from the noise and negativity around you and find instant calm. The Bubble is a shield that you visualise around you, keeping you safe inside and filled with security and confidence when it feels as if everything might overwhelm you.

In creating this bubble around yourself, you construct a space that protects and shelters you from all the noise and stress of the world as we perceive it.

So, it's a bubble that filters the stuff that you don't want to reach you. For example, if your boss or a colleague at work is annoying or difficult, you can imagine that person far away outside the bubble. If you're finding it difficult to shut off the noise from your family or your worries about money, you find that space and nobody and no worry can filter through. It's a way to put all the things that cause you stress outside, while you have your vital space within and around you that no one can invade, that is always yours. It allows you to own your power again and take a step back from your daily life and problems. It doesn't block you from connecting to the outside and receiving love and positivity; it is more a filter from stressors. It's also a space that gives you a time of non-reaction or to think before you react to something.

To start, the most important thing you can do to make your practice effective is to have a clear intention first. Take a few moments to breathe easily and prepare yourself by acknowledging that you're going to do something that will transform your present state, whether a chaotic mind or agitated feelings in the chest. As usual, let yourself be guided into the practice without preconceived ideas about what you are going to feel or find in it. Once you have reached the sophroliminal state you will build your bubble. Let it come to you and trust your consciousness in showing you the way. You will spend time feeling the calmness and clarity of being within your bubble, before you finish the exercise.

The Supertool: The Bubble 🔊

We begin with the tratac and the standing short Foundation Practice, activating calmness during its last part.

1. In the Pharaoh posture, breathing calmly and easily, visualise your own bubble. Think about how it looks, whether it is large or small, close to your body or very big around you, transparent or coloured. Take the time to visualise how it would look and let it create itself on your inner screen, feeling it around you. Everyone's will be different – let your body and mind lead you to create your own bubble: its size, its colour, its feel.

2. Now, keep imagining the bubble all around you and tune into the presence of calmness in your systems. All your stressors are outside and separate from you, and can't come close to you while you have the bubble. Experience how it feels to be in that bubble, feeling calm and secure, and giving you the space you need.

3. Take a few moments to look at the bubble all around you. In your mind, look up and down, left and right and feel the air around you and how peaceful and light it is.

4. Enjoy the feeling of being within your bubble for a while, before you return from the visualisation.

5. At the end, back in the sitting relaxed posture, pause and inhale all the positives of the exercise, remembering how it felt within your body. Take the time you need to return to the presence of your body, feel your feet on the floor and become fully present before opening your eyes.

During any Sophrology exercise, especially the supertools, you may be confronted with tensions. Your bubble might be difficult to create initially or you may find yourself dwelling on the stresses and tensions that invade you. Just acknowledge and let go by using a tension relax (page 29) and carry on focusing on the visualisation. Remember that you do not need to achieve anything in this practice. Repeat as many times as necessary. Don't forget your phenodescription.

The Bubble 'On the Go'

Remember, once you have performed this full practice a few times, you will be able to form your bubble easily in your mind when you visualise it, and the feelings and sensations it creates will become familiar. That means that if you're out and about and feel a rising sense of panic at everything happening around you or all the demands being placed upon you, you can take a few moments to breathe deeply, recall your bubble and you will naturally connect with that sense of calm and security within yourself and your own space. Instant peace!

Releasing Stress and Anger

Whether we are angry or stressed about a major situation or just the accumulation of small problems surrounding our daily life, stress and repressed anger is a real issue for a huge number of people, and is something that stays in the body, causing long-term issues. As I said earlier, my osteopathy training and experience taught me that 'the body never lies'. People feel somewhat liberated when they visit a practitioner for bodywork. There's something about the bond of trust created and, I think, the fact that there is often little eye contact, which lends itself to people choosing to unburden themselves emotionally. So many times as I worked on physical tensions and misalignments I heard about a person's mental and emotional blockages and worries. I saw so many people with their emotional tension and anxiety manifested in the physical body. These 'symptoms' ranged from back and neck issues, headaches and chest pains and erratic heartbeat to exhaustion, digestive problems and numerous infections and general illness. (I could write a much longer list here!)

Stress

At the heart of Sophrology is the mind–body connection and learning how to listen to what our body is telling us about our mental state. It is a great step forward that it is now generally accepted that stress and anxiety can cause or exacerbate physical ailments. The current conversations about treating the emotional cause of physical problems, and the interest in mindfulness and meditation, are a welcome approach to introducing regular mental healthcare into our lives as a way of protecting our physical health as well.

Obviously, the psychological effects of chronic emotional stress are also life-changing. On a simple level, being placed in a constant and ongoing state of 'high-alert' is linked to procrastination, concentration issues, negative cycles of thought, mood changes, insomnia and social anxiety – all issues that complicate everyday life, social interactions and personal relationships in a manner that further compounds stress levels. It does feel sometimes, through my practice, that huge swathes of the population are continuously living with low- to medium-level pressure brought on by the demands of the modern workplace and the issues of balancing family life and work – for women feeling that they should be 'having it all', but also for men in terms of their role in twenty-first century life. Taken to the extreme, or if endured over a period of time, stress can lead to more long-term issues such as heart problems, diabetes, depression or burnout. This is serious.

Anger

Anger is common and normal. It is one of our basic emotions – like sadness, joy or fear. But somehow it has a very bad press. I rarely have a client who sits down and tells me she or he feels angry, although everything they might describe or analyse sounds as if they are. Anger is often repressed or expressed in an out-of-control way, but I welcome it as an emotion that must be processed like any other. Like all other emotions, anger is not negative or positive, it just is – and needs to be acknowledged. Anger is necessary so that when we feel threatened or disrespected we can react. It helps us realise when we need to set up boundaries. In a physical threat, it helps us find the energy to fight for our life. So it has huge destructive potential and this is probably why we collectively find it harder to deal with than other emotions. The way to deal with it positively is to feel it, live it and, like all other emotions, it will pass if we don't fight it. It is not socially acceptable to scream at your boss for what they just said or start punching someone because they inadvertently pushed you on the street. It is all about knowing what to do with this feeling that can be so overwhelming, and to channel it so it is useful. When we are at peace with our angry feelings and able to deal with them positively, we are more likely to find non-violent ways to express ourselves, and to communicate with others to find a way where our needs are met. It is when anger isn't conscious or given the chance to be processed that imbalances occur. When anger becomes a state of being rather than an emotion.

Similar to stress, anger is an emotion that stimulates immediate physical sensations in the body. The message to the brain that causes the anger sparks a release of hormones (mostly adrenaline and testosterone) and a spike in heart rate that affects numerous systems in the body. Basically, as with stress, it's causing your body systems to work differently, to prioritise some things over others, and it's not a long-term state of health that your body can endure. I have noted on numerous occasions with clients who believed they were suffering with anxiety that once they were able to connect with their feelings of anger and process them, their level of anxiety was strongly diminished.

So, long-term stress and anger are hugely detrimental to all aspects of our life and we need to stop these effects. But how? Do we have the power to replace our stressful boss (unlikely) or to move our home closer to the school/station/work to make daily life easier? Sadly not. The key to coping with these destructive emotions is to acknowledge and process them in order to let them go.

Inner Resource: Letting Go

I think that one of the most powerful aphorisms or prayers is the one often referred to as the Serenity Prayer: 'Grant us the serenity to accept the things we cannot change, the courage to change the things we can and the wisdom to know the difference.' It's so easy to forget that plenty of our stresses can't be changed or taken away by us; we don't have that control. And it is this key problem at the heart of our anxiety and anger – situations that we cannot control or change and what we can do to release ourselves from their negative effects and change the perception we have of them. In other words – learning to let go.

It's a simple concept, letting go (and not to be trivialised by the Disney song) but surprisingly difficult to enact. Remember that stress and anger are our own body's reaction to a situation, words spoken to us, or the behaviour of those around us. And sometimes this prompt has happened a while earlier, or even years ago. It's very easy to *allow* things to cause us great distress and harm – maybe it's the unfairness of it all, sometimes it's the lack of control. And while we are busy responding, or are distracted, we aren't able to do anything to improve the situation or to move on with our lives – we are stuck. It's not helped by the fact that we're so busy 'doing' and trying to keep our life going that we tend to keep our emotions tightly within. So we hold all this negative stuff and our body fills with it more and more. Imagine ourselves as a saucepan filled with a liquid, boiling away on a stove, with hot liquid being added – getting fuller and fuller, and in danger of spilling over. But if our body was able to acknowledge and process all this stress and anger at the time of the trigger, or regularly when it began to feel overwhelming, it wouldn't be able to build up and cause damage.

The Supertool: The Pump 🔊))

And that is what we do in Sophrology to gain balance and calm – we regain control of the situation by acknowledging what we are feeling and releasing the tension to restore calm and balance. In Sophrology we can acknowledge our feelings in the body too. Often I will ask, 'In which system do you feel your emotion today?' And we start by working on that system. I might ask, 'What is the colour/shape of your anger?' Just so people connect with a different aspect of themselves.

Now we've come across this exercise before – it's the Second System exercise from our Level 1 practice on page 113. It's such a powerful exercise and one of the moves that my clients come back to time and time again, as part of their practice and when dealing with a tricky moment in their daily life.

1. Begin with the tratac and short Foundation Practice standing.
2. Then stand relaxed, arms at your sides, breathing easily. Take time to notice how you feel mentally, emotionally and physically, perhaps thinking about where your stress or anger feeling is mostly located.
3. Clench your hands into fists at your side. Exhale through your mouth, and inhale, then hold your breath and 'pump' your shoulders up and down, keeping your arms straight, for several seconds. Then exhale. As you release the arms and hands, use it as a symbolic gesture of a letting go in relation to what you have noted earlier. And just let it go!
4. Listen briefly for sensation. Then repeat.
5. Again, take a moment for a seated integration pause, tuning into positive sensation, your vital power or a sense of calm.

The Pump is a wonderfully liberating and energising movement that can be done energetically (especially helpful if you are processing anger) or more calmly if you prefer. It is also hugely effective for processing a range of emotions that we would like to let go – such as frustration, tiredness or fear.

The Pump 'On the Go'

Once you have practised the full exercise in the sophroliminal state several times, you can use this tool for an instant release of negative energy, for example after a phone call that you've found really stressful or if you find yourself shouting at someone over something unimportant. Just taking one minute to realise that you're going through this emotion yourself, and doing The Pump, allows you to let the steam go so that you're more ready to confront the problem.

'Empowering! I feel it gives me a toolbox to deal with things to really take the power back.' Anne

Confidence and Success

Confidence and success are attributes that we often deem other people to have but not ourselves. Sometimes this becomes a factor in the way we live our life, the choices we make or the way we view our past. It doesn't help that lots of self-help talks about 'fake it till you make it', and advises how you can 'learn' confidence. It perpetuates the theory that it's a skill, rather than a power that we all have within us. Look at a toddler or small child – 'fearless' is often a word we use to describe them as they have a predilection for the nearest set of stairs, furniture to climb or something to 'explore'.

When I was pregnant I had great hopes for my birth – it was going to be as natural and easy as possible. But when it didn't go according to my plan and I had to have a c-section, I could have been left with huge disappointment and a sense of failure. The intense preparation I had done with Sophrology helped me to bounce back quickly, physically and mentally. I was able to access the deeper meaning of my experience and focus on the positives: notably the fact that I had a happy, healthy and wonderful baby. I think it would have been much harder to have confidence in myself and to see the situation as a success and a happy one without my Sophrology. I was able to trust that, even if everything didn't go exactly to plan, then I'd still gone through a life-changing moment and experienced something of worth, and built my resilience through the experience.

And here, we look at ways to tune in again to that innate confidence and inner strength, and to evaluate what they mean to us. Knowing yourself and being truly present in yourself is the easiest way to 'find' your confidence. When we are too much in our head with our thoughts, limiting beliefs, fears and emotions – which are often framed around the past or the future – we get lost and are not sure who to listen to or what to do for the best. Being in a state of balance and true to yourself allows you to make decisions that are right for you and to stand tall and be proud of them.

Inner Resource: Confidence

In Sophrology, confidence is linked to trust: trusting in yourself and in knowing who you are, your authentic self. It's also about trusting yourself in terms of setting out your path to success and your future – and understanding that if you can free yourself from a lack of confidence and listen to your body and your inner self, you will end up in a much better place. It is also gaining an inner trust that things always turn out well in the end. A sense of deep hope for the future. A trust in the future.

Traditionally we talk about our subconscious inner voice, intuition or instincts (which we might think of as coming from our brain) in terms of our body – our 'sixth sense', a 'feeling in our body' or our 'water', and a 'gut instinct' (interesting given the current discussion about the links between the gut and the brain and the importance of the gut's microbiome as a 'second brain'). In Sophrology, you build up your confidence, and success, through increasing your awareness of the body. As you build up your basic practice, you are relearning that you have a body on which you can lean and anchor yourself at any moment. Remember that your body is your friend and your 'vehicle for life'. Confidence becomes something we are, we feel and we live in our daily life rather than something we need to think about or make an effort about. It is a way to go through life with a positive outlook, looking out for the best in a situation and trusting that we are able to do or be what we want. The practice of Level 1 is a very good tool to start building these feelings of confidence (or reconnecting with them, as confidence is part of all of us already). Sometimes it just needs to be reignited in relation to a challenging situation. And it is exactly what we present in this chapter. Think about the situation where your confidence is triggered. It may be linked to work, relationships, health or identity. What would it change in your situation if you could be totally confident?

Part of the Sophrology path is asking yourself and uncovering what you most value in life (Level 4). You may realise that through your practice your definition of success will shift. What feels like success to you? What makes you feel happy, motivated and content? It is common for my clients who have created a great career and reached what they consider as a success to realise that actually what they valued so much is now making them highly stressed. How can they enjoy their daily life and cope with the pressure that often goes with the success that they wanted? Be bold with your success. Don't be afraid to aim high, as you will be surprised where the power of Sophrology can take you. I used to be anxious about school and exams and I wish I had known that through my Sophrology practice I would go into my A levels with my hands in my pockets in the mornings, so relaxed and happy that this day was finally here. My mum was worried and said, 'I have never seen you so relaxed, are you sure you will be OK?' Years later, if someone had told me I would have been able to change my profession, change country and live the life I aspired to in London, it would have seemed like a dream. Be careful what you visualise as it often comes true . . .! And if it doesn't, the fact you have prepared for success will help you be creative and resilient whatever the outcome. It becomes a state of mind rather than something that is attached to a particular outcome.

That's why confidence is so important. By trusting what you deeply feel and aspire to, you are often able to adjust the situation so it is more in line with your levels of energy and capacity. It's about valuing yourself, your time and well-being in a system that too often does not.

Confidence and success are often judged around what you do and how you perform at specific events, be they exams, work presentations or social occasions, and Sophrology has several tools that are specifically created to bring you an instant confidence boost in preparation for an important event or when you're out and about.

For our supertool, we're going to create a visualisation going into the future to an event that has fully succeeded, creating positivity around that event. You teach yourself to 'see' beyond the event, to realise that it's not a huge mountain and that it's perfectly achievable for you. By creating a sense of success and exploring and experiencing the associated feelings surrounding this while in the sophroliminal state, we connect our body with its core strength. We allow ourselves to accept the feelings of our confident self and practise letting go of negative thoughts and feelings surrounding this situation.

We'll do a short Foundation Practice first to reach our relaxed state and connect with the body. Then, think of an event that is coming up for which you would like to increase your confidence. It doesn't have to be something major – it could be a small party that you're attending but are nervous about, a presentation you are giving to professional colleagues or a difficult conversation you need to have. You're going to visualise what it will feel like once that event is over and has been successful, how you feel now that it has happened as you wanted it to, and you are filled with joy and happiness about the results. You have set the intention for the exercise and then you remain open to what will emerge in body and mind. Try not to decide on the visualisation before going into your practice, but trust the power of consciousness to show you the way and let the images come to you. Again, it's not about 'succeeding' in the visualisation and making sure that you visualise it all perfectly, it's about engaging with the exercise and trying your best. See what comes. You may be faced with tensions and apprehensions. Acknowledge them and let them go using the tension relax (page 29) as many times as you need, as we have seen previously.

The Supertool: The Magic Picture 🔊

1. Begin with a short Foundation Practice sitting. From that deep state of relaxation, calm and connection, let's go into the visualisation.

2. With your eyes closed, in the Pharaoh posture, picture a positive image of yourself in your situation that has fully succeeded – so perhaps the day after the event when you are already in that new state of being. You have reached your goal and are beyond the stress and preparation (if it's an exam or presentation) and you have succeeded. Create the most positive image that you can of yourself in a happy state after the achievement that you wanted. Think about where you are, what time of the day it is, what you are doing or wearing, how you feel, who you are with. Being in the sophroliminal state will allow your mind to benefit from the deep relaxed state of calm and confidence you created in your body earlier, so you can be as positively creative for that situation as possible.

3. Stay with the visualisation for a little while, imagining how you would feel in yourself after the event (happy, relieved, proud of yourself) and any other actions that might occur, such as people telling you well done and that they enjoyed your presentation, or receiving a medal or certificate.

4. And finally, back in the sitting relaxed posture, come out of your visualisation with a feeling of warmth and

love, remembering how it felt within your body. Take the time you need to return to the presence of your body, feel your feet on the floor and become fully present before opening your eyes.

5. Enjoy your phenodescription now.

Some people might start the visualisation very positively and then suddenly feel a tension, and some might not even be able to do this. That's perfectly normal, so don't worry. Just use the tension relax exercise (page 29) along the way. We are trying to train the mind to open itself to positive possibilities. Notice and acknowledge how it felt for you and write it in your phenodescription after your practice. And repeat it. And as you try more, it will evolve practice after practice. You will be able to create the images you want and it will help you see the blocks that are in your mind. Maybe you realise that what you are trying to achieve is not right for you? Maybe you will identify what is holding you back from your confident future. This is a very illuminating practice.

The Magic Picture 'On the Go'

On a day when you are stressed or worried about an upcoming event, if you've practised that sense of calm and confidence connected with the presence of the body in your visualisation, you're more likely to be able to reconnect with that feeling in the moment as it's imprinted on the body sensation. It's almost as if we're 'sticking' the positive sensation into your cells, and saying that you've created this positive sensation in the mind that you can then anchor in the body. And every time you have a fear or are worried, slow your mind and your body will know it is possible. As you change your perception of how it's possible, you're more likely to succeed as you open the possibilities.

Letting Go of Negativity

Do you find yourself constantly battling negative thoughts and worries – worries about your health or weight, what people might be thinking of you or things you have said, or whether you're able to succeed in what you want? It's good to remember that very few people are as confident as they appear from the outside, but when you find yourself drowning in negativity then you need to do something about that. It's exhausting mentally and physically to deal with the barrage of noise that negativity creates. And negative thoughts also make it very difficult for you to hear your inner voice and act in a manner true to yourself, or to achieve your own personal success.

If negativity is blocking you from moving forward in life, and taking away your confidence and energy, then this exercise is for you. By clearing the barrage of negative noise, you will soon be able to focus your attention on the positive resources that you have to move yourself and your life forward. This exercise is like a symbolic act, an exercise you do to free yourself from something that is in your way.

Inner Resource: Positivity

One of the core tenets of Sophrology is its focus on the power of positivity. It's easy to get into a habit of being negative – but it has a major effect on your life and relationships. Imagine your inner negative voice like a bad friend, always around and asking you, 'Are you sure you'll be able to manage that?' or, 'Well, anyone could do that, it's not that difficult.' You wouldn't choose to spend a lot of time with someone who didn't make you feel good, so you need to try to turn your inner voice into an inspiring 'friend' who makes you feel happy and good about yourself. Think of a day when you were feeling particularly good about yourself – a day when you got up and the morning wasn't a crazy rush. Maybe you put on a new piece of clothing and felt good when you looked in the mirror. Perhaps it was one of those days when your morning routine or commute went to plan. It's easy to underestimate how much that optimism changed your day – how a good mood and feeling positive made life easier for you, and turned the small problems that happen every day of our life into funny stories that you tell someone later and laugh about. Your perception of the event or day is completely changed.

The more integrated and united we are and the more positivity we feel and experience, the easier it is to feel positive. This is not being positive at any price, not like a warrior who thinks that the only way forward is to be positive. We have to understand that life has its ups and downs – it's not about cultivating denial of what goes wrong, or what feels wrong or painful.

As we regularly practise and move towards more harmony and calm, we naturally develop a more positive mindset, an ability to be in the moment and enjoy what there is to enjoy, greater gratitude, and a sense of confidence in our resources and hope that things will go well or for the better. It's not something we force upon ourselves with willpower but rather something we become through the practice of Sophrology.

Here we use an empowering exercise called The Bag to rid ourselves of negative thoughts, emotions and situations and clear the associated weight and tension. Once we are fully grounded and present in our body we are going to visualise a bag in front of us, and we are going to place all of our negative thoughts or concerns in it, one by one. You can put in all the negative things in your mind – emotions such as anger or resentment, frustration or hurt, a negative belief that stops you from achieving what you could, or something hurtful that a friend says to you. (You can't put people in the bag!) You may also feel a heaviness or tension in your body in relation to the situation you are in, so symbolically add it in there too. And then you are going to 'crush' the bag with your hands and stomp on it with your feet, reducing the contents to dust. Finally, you 'pick up' the dust, exhale and send it to the universe and ask for it to be transformed. So, it's a symbolic act that allows your brain to acknowledge and process these negative thoughts and emotions, using your intention and physical movements to effect the change. It can be performed forcefully if you have lots of pent-up negative energy, using your voice to add impact to the movements, or it can be done calmly. It's also a great tool to teach to children to deal effectively with events that have troubled them. Remember that everything can be symbolically placed in this bag except people, as we are crushing this bag!

The Supertool: The Bag 🔊

1. We begin with the tratac and short Foundation Practice standing.
2. Tune into a sense of confidence that you are able to transform negative beliefs, emotion, worries and tension in your body – anything in the way of you getting on with your goal, plan and serenity – breathe in the confidence.
3. With eyes closed, stand about a metre-and-a-half in front of a wall and imagine that there is a target on the wall, and on that target is hanging a bag. And this bag can look however you want it to look. You can put into the bag everything that bothers you – whether it's an emotion such as anger or regret, a belief that you can't stop going around your head or some occasion on

which you felt disrespected. You can put in everything except actual people – but you can put in what the person has said and how it has made your feel. Use one hand to hold the bag and the other to place each item inside it as you exhale, carefully naming and acknowledging each item either out loud or in your head as you place it inside. When you have finished, close the bag.

4. Next, you assume a kind of karate position – with one leg in front of the other and one hand in a fist 'crushing' the bag. Three times you inhale then exhale and hit the bag with one hand and then the other hand, then with both hands together. Then visualise all the pieces of the bag falling on the floor.

5. To fully destroy the bag and its contents, you then stomp quickly with both feet on the spot on the floor where the bag remnants 'fell', to reduce the bag to dust.

6. Inhale and reach down to collect the dust, then you exhale and stand up, and 'send' the dust to the universe asking for it to be transformed.

7. All the way through keep connected to what you feel. The moves can feel quite violent if you are very upset. You can use your voice too – an 'aah' sound if that helps – but don't hurt yourself and listen to your body.

8. To finish, invite into yourself something positive like peace or self-love or confidence or gratitude that you are alive and hopeful, placing your hands on top of each other over your heart and letting things settle in

your mind and body. And then take a moment to sit down and integrate your experience by observing the sensations in your body here and now until you hopefully feel calm again.

9. Enjoy your phenodescription.

Using the power of feeling grounded, this move is extremely effective at bringing relief from negative thoughts and patterns and, like a child having a tantrum about something they don't like, it is extremely liberating to let go of yourself and trample on the things that are hurting you!

The dust represents the negativity that is transformed as you exhale and release it to the universe – offering it as a gift to the universe to transform. It's as if you are not alone and, by offering it to the universe with that clear intention in mind, it will help you achieve your goals in return.

You will be physically tired after this exercise, as you're releasing a lot of tension that has been weighing you down. It's important to do this exercise in a calm environment where and when you feel safe to show your emotion. Some people are naturally more expressive and less worried about releasing their emotions and using their voice to let go of all that stress and negativity that blocks them. It's a symbolic act and the brain needs those times of acknowledgment and transformation. Again, it brings together intention, movement and breathing to bring about a profound effect on consciousness.

The Bag 'On the Go'

If you are unable to do this exercise in full and need some relief from negativity on the go, there is a quick way to ease your emotions.

Simply tune into the negative sensation, thought or difficult emotion and inhale, bringing one hand clenched into a fist towards you, and as you exhale through your mouth push the hand quickly away from you and open your hand as if you are letting go of the negativity. Then simply place that hand over your heart and invite something positive into your heart – a calming, loving and relaxing thought or intention.

Like all on the go Sophrology exercises, it will work best if you have practised the full versions in the sophroliminal state already.

Instant Calm

Now, who wouldn't benefit from or wish for a way to find instant serenity at a time of chaos or extreme emotion? The Reflex Sign is one of the most popular supertools that I and many of my clients use all the time to signal to the brain to trigger calm. When you're feeling emotionally threatened by a situation, it's a strength and protection and an extra grounding in the moment. It can be good to use before a difficult event, or even during a stressful meeting or an exam, if you feel as if you're losing your concentration or even if you're on the tube and feeling claustrophobic or anxious.

It is something that you train your brain to do beforehand in your own time and at a time of calm – you use a small hand movement and link it with a sensation of deep calm and happiness. Then, because you have created these links in your brain between the hand movement and the state of being while in deep relaxation, you will be able to activate the signal for calm on the spot when you are out and about.

Inner Resource: Resilience

Resilience or grit doesn't sound very life-changing, but in Sophrology we recognise this attribute as crucial to positivity and the ability to find balance in life. We will always have bad days and suffer knocks to our confidence, but the ability to get back up and carry on is a crucial part of emotional maturity. Again, it comes from 'being' rather than 'doing'. When we find the time and space from our busy daily lives to stay grounded and centred, and working on the connection between our body and mind, we retain the ability to separate our core self from the events happening around us. By allowing that separation between our own being and the people and circumstances around us, we gain a healthy perspective from which we are able to acknowledge and accept circumstances more easily.

Remember that what happens in life is only a little about what happens to you, and mostly about how you react in return. So if you're going into a difficult situation you will be able to tune in and have more clarity in order to find a solution rather than being overwhelmed. If you learn to calm your body and be able to feel when you're stressed, then you're less likely to act on anxiety, and the stress levels decreasing help you to think more clearly and listen more carefully to what is happening emotionally. Managing your emotions is the way to be more resilient.

The Reflex Sign is instant calm. It's a way to connect in the moment with a positive sensation – calm or confidence perhaps – that you want to achieve on the spot. It's like being able to stay connected no matter what is going on around you. The principle of the tool is that at a non-stressful time, you do the key techniques so that you are fully present in your body and in the deep state of relaxation, and then go through the Reflex Sign exercise. Repeat this several times to 'create' the tool – in this case, pressing together your thumb and fingertips of your first two fingers. Then you will be able to use your reflex sign whenever you need. You are practising this outside of the time of stress in order to be able to activate the gesture in the time of stress. The key is to take a small, simple body movement that you can attach to the intention of the body. Using your fingers is usually very good – and you can even do it in your pocket in a meeting, say, as no one will see you do this. But do adapt this tool if you need to.

The Supertool: The Reflex Sign 🔊

1. After the tratac and short Foundation Practice sitting, breathe deeply.

2. Take a moment to acknowledge and feel the calm and relaxation in your body. It may manifest as heaviness, or you feeling centred or whole. Tune into your inner screen, and create an image of a landscape you like, or use the happy place we mentioned earlier, a place outdoors where you are completely relaxed and at peace. Visualise it and use all of your senses to immerse yourself in it. Think of how the air there feels on your skin – maybe there is a lovely scent, or a relaxing sound you can hear. And then absorb deeply how it makes you feel – calm, happy, relaxed – to further enhance that positive body and mind state.

3. Once you are very calm and comfortable inside your visualisation, inhale and bring together the thumb and the fingertips of the first two fingers. Press them together firmly as you simultaneously tune into the calm sensation in your body and see your landscape. When you exhale, relax further into that lovely sensation and image. And then say something like, 'Every time I press my fingers together it will instantly connect me with the deep sense of relaxation and calm that I am experiencing right now.' And then do it again, pressing thumb and fingers together, inhaling, exhaling and release. And on the exhale, you

160

release your fingers and release your body even deeper into the state of calm.

4. Repeat this again twice while focusing on the scene of calm and the relaxation in your body.

5. Finally, finish and observe your sensation until you are ready to do your slow return.

6. Write your phenodescription.

'I do the clench and the release and then it's just as if everything goes away. It clears my mind and I feel so much more relaxed.' Benjamin

The Reflex Sign 'On the Go'

This is a very simple exercise, but its success depends on a good Foundation Practice so that the person is very relaxed and in the sophroliminal state, as that's where we can make those reflex connections between the brain, the body sensation and the gesture. We call it the Reflex Sign as we use the reflexes of the system that are natural to us (like the Pavlovian learnt reflex of the bell and the dog, using natural pathways of association) and the ability of the brain to connect a gesture with calm, so that every time we do that we will reach that state of calm.

As you have seen in Benjamin's story, this exercise is meant to be used on the go when you need it. Whether you are about to serve on the tennis court or can feel the stress building up during a stressful phone conversation, you can use your Reflex Sign to change your response to your situation.

Sleep and Managing Energy

Everybody feels differently about sleep. Some need lots whereas others can survive for a long time on very little. A few of us are lucky enough to sleep deeply no matter what is happening in our lives, but others have never slept well and struggle with it all their life. Add to this the pressures of looking after babies and children or lots of travel or shift-work and it can be a huge influencer on our daily life and our ability to function properly.

Sleep deprivation has many consequences, from tired-ness to muscle pain, from a stressed mind to feeling more sensitive, depressed and irritable emotionally, to compen-sating with over-eating (with resulting weight gain), using alcohol to fall asleep and drinking coffee and smoking to stay awake during the day. What we all agree on is that sleep is one of the essential pillars of good health along with good nutrition and movement. It rejuvenates the body and mind.

With sleep problems, it is always a good idea to visit your GP first to get a formal medical opinion. Whatever the causes of your difficulties in sleeping and whether the issues are chronic or sporadic, the aim with Sophrology is to create the best conditions for body and mind to access more and better sleep.

A Calm Sleep Environment

The sleeping state should be seen as a sacred state as it is so important. Starting with your sleeping environment, think about how to make it best suited to a full restful night's sleep. Ensuring you have a comfortable bed, a de-cluttered space, the right temperature (not too warm) and good blinds to screen out morning light are obvious things to consider. Having a room with no screens and of course making sure your work files or house accounts are not by your bedside will also help! Have in your bedroom only objects that make you feel happy and peaceful, and try to keep the area clutter-free.

Think about a simple routine you could have every night to prepare you for bed. Make sure you stop watching screens a good 90 minutes before bedtime and think about what you would like to do instead. Choose reading a book, taking a bath, talking to a friend or listening to music – so that you are giving your body and mind a chance to start relaxing as you approach bedtime.

Thanks to your Sophrology practice (Foundation and Level 1), you will also start to be more in tune with the signs your body or mind give you to let you know you need to sleep. Finding your body clock is key for a restful sleep. You would already have learnt how to relax and control your stress levels throughout the day, so that when the end of the day approaches you are in a more balanced state. Being aware of this and repeating your routine, it will be easier to discover the natural rhythms of your body around sleeping and waking. Think of how you would help a baby or small child 'learn' how to sleep, and treat yourself with similar care. Learn more about what works for your body and your life, and find a sleep routine that helps signal to and prepare your body for sleep.

More than with any other Sophrology practice, the key for the sleep technique is regularity; it needs to be daily, even if just for 10 minutes. Simply practising the Foundation and Level 1 exercises will be a huge help to your sleep issues, for a start. The Foundation Practice will help you slow your brain – a state of recuperation that is greatly needed if you are lacking sleep, as well as enabling you to reconnect with your ability to relax, which is key to falling asleep. The Bubble supertool (page 135) is also a good one to practise for a while. You could even do it lying down if you are too tired for a standing practice. These exercises will help you connect with more confidence in your body, a body that you may not trust any more in its ability to achieve the state of sleep or to maintain it for a long time. It will help you start learning how to focus and let go of the unnecessary mind activity or worries you may have. The Level 1 practice will release all the tensions you accumulate (even without noticing) throughout your day. Conscious and unconscious worries and tensions play a big part in how well we sleep, and practising Level 1 will help you become aware of and clear of what is in the way of your relaxation and restorative moments. Knowing your body better through Level 1 and tuning into its positive resources will help you restore that lost confidence in your ability to sleep.

There are many ways we can help sleep problems with Sophrology, so it was difficult to choose one exercise here for this book (see page 135 for a couple more options). It is about preparing and reprogramming your body and mind in a positive way for sleep and includes a visualisation as well as choosing a word that will be the gatekeeper of your peaceful sleeping state.

This exercise needs to be 'practised' in the daytime, when you are fully awake. You will choose a word that can be the gatekeeper of your night, and your sacred space of sleep. What sensation would be comforting or empowering to actually be in that space of sleep? Any anxiety or disruption that is compromising this time of sleep can be kept out of that sacred space of sleep by the gatekeeper. And the word you have decided on will be activated by the breath. As you breathe automatically during the night, it will be reinforced in your consciousness through your breath. Choose a word that is meaningful for you, and that gives you confidence in your ability to fall asleep and stay asleep. You will then be guided to visualise the end of your day in the most positive way, creating images about your bedtime routine working perfectly, how falling asleep looks and feels as it happens smoothly, and synchronising your out breath with the gatekeeper word that you use to see yourself falling asleep. (And if a worry, a disturbing noise or any other potential disturbance to our peaceful state of sleep arises, we would simply use the out breath and the word to go back to sleep.) In the same way that the reflex sign works during the day, that word with the out breath is for the night. The visualisation carries on through us sleeping well, and waking up in a positive state the next morning to go through our daily activities in a calm and happy way until the routine starts again preparing for sleep. And it's that simple.

Supertool: The Sleep Gatekeeper 🔊

1. Sit down, and do your tratac and short Foundation Practice. Then invite the word that can be the gatekeeper of your night, and your sacred space of sleep. It can be anything like 'calm', 'relaxation' or 'confidence'.

2. Then inhale the word, and on the exhale you will invite it in to your systems. The next step is a visualisation around creating the routine you will do every night before you go to bed. See yourself going through the routine in the most positive way and then falling asleep as easily as possible, going through the night easily, waking up refreshed and motivated to start your day and going through the next day in the way you wish, feeling happy and balanced.

3. Throughout that visualisation of the routine, regularly connect with your breath and the chosen word,

reinforcing its power in keeping safe the sacred space of sleep. Then the visualisation ends with the start of your next night routine – a 24-hour visualisation.

4. Finish the visualisation by inhaling a sense of confidence in your ability to sleep and exhale it through your body. Take a moment to listen to sensation before your slow return.

5. Write your phenodescription.

During this visualisation, if something comes up that is not comfortable, if you find it impossible to visualise this success, or if your body is aching, simply inhale, tense the body and exhale. These are all part of the experience of Sophrology and are not to be denied but embraced.

Repeat as many times as is needed and remember that by repeating your exercise your images and sensations will evolve, making you more and more able to find positive imaging and calm through the experience. You are actively inviting your natural inner resource of sleep to balance and strengthen. I can't stress enough that repetition of the practice during the daytime (and any Sophrology practice) is key to changing your sleep patterns for good.

Extra Tools for Change

As we have already said, many Sophrology exercises can be adapted for different aims. Practising Level 1 exercises alongside your supertools will simply make everything more powerful as you will be even more deeply in tune with body and mind. Remember that Sophrology should become yours after you have understood and learnt it, so don't be afraid to experiment. Here are a few ideas for new ways in which the practice can improve your life:

The **Body Halves** exercise (the Level 1 megasystem exercise on page 120) is a wonderful tool to build for success and confidence and can be practised before any visualisation to be more in tune with your body.

Use the **Head Rotation** (the Level 1 System 1 exercise on page 112) to oxygenate your brain, and find calm and focus through your body awareness. It can be done before The Bubble exercise to encourage further clarity and headspace.

For improved sleep, the **Level 1 practice** on page 108 performed regularly will make a significant difference. Also, use the tension relax and monitor your breathing through-out the day with the diagnostic breathing exercise to avoid accumulating tensions.

Use **The Bellows** (Level 1 System 4 on page 117) and **The Shoulder Pump** on page 113 and finish with **The Bag** exercise on page 154 if your emotions are still all over the place!

Use **The Windmill** exercise on page 114 and a creative visualisation of a positive event in your future to let go of an anxious state.

See what I mean. Once you have practised on a regular basis, you can become your own Sophrologist!

CASE STUDY: **MAGUELONNE**
– 'NOW WAS THE TIME TO LISTEN TO THIS BODY.'

Maguelonne, 57, is a psychotherapist, and a wife, mum and grandma. She came to me because of fibromyalgia – a very painful state of the body, which had been diagnosed seven years before. She was constantly in pain, and extremely tired. She was also struggling with stress due to her husband suffering from health problems. She had decided to leave her job to look after herself and get better. Being a psychotherapist and having done psychoanalysis since her forties, she had already been on a long path of self-discovery.

The fact that the sessions are recorded is very helpful. It's good for supporting me at home and it starts the energy going.

In that first session, I remember what was really telling was to associate a gesture with an intention. I did The Bag exercise to put all my worries inside – it freed me. It was very powerful. The second exercise was The Bubble. We practised before I went back to France so I could keep my own space and set limits in relation to the outside world. That helps a lot as well. And using the tension relax associated with breathing, becoming aware of my body tensing and relaxing, was very helpful as well.

I'm becoming more and more aware that my body belongs to me. When I used to go to the doctor, I would feel a little uneasy and threatened and not satisfied with that relationship, as if my body belonged to someone else. Now my body belongs to me.

Dominique also helped me to connect my experience with my body, kind of embodying what I was saying. There is a saying in France, something like 'shoemakers always have the worst shoes'. As a psychotherapist, it's difficult for me to connect with my body and I need help to connect that experience. I understand the process of psychoanalysis in providing the space for words and meaning, but the fact that we integrate the body in this experience allows the person to listen to their body sensation and warnings, and to the message that comes from the body to empower them to find a way into their experience.

It makes a big difference in my daily life. I used to be 'head only'. When something happened, I was very good at making links about what caused it – like 'this is to do with my mum or my dad ...' Now I try not to do that and to connect instead with how I feel in that moment. That is a big change for me. I ask 'What do I need now?' and I trust and listen that it's my body that will send me the message, not the mind. And in creating *The Bubble*, I realised that I don't need to sit there and absorb everything that people tell me. I realised I can say, 'Stop now', or, 'We're not going to do this now. Maybe we can meet later to discuss it.' I'm setting clear limits for myself. Doing the tension relax in the morning helps me to reconnect with that ability to decide for myself what is good for me. I'm trying to be centred in my body in the experience instead of trying to control the body with the mind. Just the simple fact that there is a message coming through from the body allows me to let go.

So it's finding the balance between being a wife, a mum, a grandma and a therapist. And allowing myself to give enough importance to me to take care of myself. I knew that theoretically, and in my mind, but it was only when I connected with my body that suddenly it became a reality. That I could actually accept that. When I came to Dominique with my fibromyalgia, my body was screaming, saying how painful it was. So I told myself that now was the time to listen to this body that was screaming for help.

And I noticed how fast this has changed. I spent years and years dealing with understanding and analysing the how and why of my story. Now I can let go of my mind, just enjoy life being present in the body. I've done meditation before . . . and with meditation I was very much in the mind. Meditation is like opening a window a little, whereas Sophrology is like opening the door wide . . .

PART 3

Your Future With Sophrology

10 Minutes to Build Your Positive Future

In this chapter, we are given the opportunity to understand the dual nature of Sophrology. Our supertools are the way we find a happier and calmer daily life, and now we will look at the power of Sophrology to transform our relationship with our future and effect long-term change. Deep within our body and mind is hidden what we really aspire to. Connected to ourselves in the sophroliminal state, we are given a chance to prepare for our future in a positive way, to be in touch with what we value most, what truly supports our existence or inner purpose.

Sophrology doesn't impose anything, it encourages the freedom of each individual in finding meaning. Do you value family, freedom, love, simplicity, nature, success, spirituality, respect, connection, community, sport, friendship, health? What truly motivates you to wake up in the morning? Sophrology helps us incarnate this innermost sentiment and look at our reality with new eyes. Below you will find powerful 10-minute practices to transform your life using Level 2 creative visualisations, and a taste of Levels 2, 3 and 4 of Sophrology.

As a practitioner, I find it hugely rewarding to see the changes effected by working towards the future in Sophrology.

This work is incredibly powerful. When you visualise the past or the future, to the brain and nervous system it's as if you are directly there, experiencing it. This is one reason why revisiting traumatic times from the past is so difficult, despite knowing that they are behind us. It still prompts a physiological response. So we do a positive visualisation into the future – a futurisation – to prepare the body and mind for the future. We stimulate our inner resources here and now for the future event, so that we can bring greater creativity, confidence or clarity to the event. When we live that event, we go through it with a greater awareness and presence, and reduced anxiety, as our brain has already 'experienced' it.

In Sophrology, visualisation is a power that is rooted in the mind and supported by the body. In other words, the Foundation Practice we do at the beginning of a session and the fact that we have learnt to be more in tune with our body through sensations, notably through our Level 1 practice, informs our projection with the mind. As we are calm and centred in our body, we support the mind in creating meaningful images that are truly connected to our essence and the power of consciousness. The practice of futurisation helps us to feel confident and positive as well as opening up our brain to new possibilities.

In this section, we explore how you can:

Create a Happy Daily Life (page 177)
Enjoy a Bright Future (page 181)
Be Empowered by Your Past (page 185)
Explore Your Life Purpose (page 187)

Create a Happy Daily Life

We all have a daily life filled with lots of things 'to do', and some of this stuff may not be not the most exciting. Our days may be filled with tasks that are essential but hold no joy, and that feel repetitive and unappreciated, or perhaps we spend much of our day at our desk in a job that pays the bills and is needed but brings no spark to life, or where our own self is not nourished. Here, we have an opportunity to take back control of how we feel in a positive way for large parts of our normal life and to explore the potential of every day, to shift our mind and open ourselves to new possibilities.

This is a very special and important practice to cultivate positive change through examining the detail of our daily life. We are going to look at the mindset of our perfect day. Well, maybe not our perfect day – there aren't likely to be desert islands involved – but we are going to create in our mind our 'best day' and look at how it could feel. Perhaps you normally live a life filled with stress and activity and wish to live your daily life more calmly, or maybe it's about a state of confidence that you want to be in going through your daily life.

In this practice we will choose to bring more positivity, joy, happiness, calm or whatever we need more of into our everyday. So, it's about going into the future – a comfortable future in terms of timing: ideally it would be the next day, or at least in the next week. We will do a futurisation by creating images on our inner screen for an entire day, cultivating positivity for our future daily life in all the tasks that we have to do and the places and people that form our normal life. But we do this with rose-tinted glasses on, as if it really is the best version possible of our typical day from the moment we get up until we go to bed. Don't plan anything beforehand with your thinking mind. Simply go into this exercise with as much positivity as possible and see what comes out of it. Once you are in your sophroliminal state, you will ask yourself, 'How would I like to feel in my day tomorrow?' In this way our whole consciousness will give us the answer rather than the purely rational part of ourselves.

As you 'revisit' your daily life in a different way you are allowed to adapt it as you want. So, if you normally struggle to wake up and get out of bed and normally your bedroom is messy with all your clothes and possessions everywhere, it puts your mind into a state that is not clear and prepared for the day. In the visualisation, view yourself getting calmly out of bed feeling rested, and look around yourself at your room in the way you want it to be. Think about how you want to eat your breakfast and what it could be – if you want it to be a healthy meal eaten at the table rather than a cereal bar on the train, then find the time in your perfect day to make that happen. Then think about your morning and how you spend it. In your visualisation, maybe see yourself travelling calmly to work and having a productive day – working efficiently and creatively, juggling your priorities well and communicating with colleagues about mutual projects. If you are spending the day at leisure or caring for children or adults, ensure that you build elements into the day that are personally fulfilling. You may be surprised that your ideal day suddenly takes the form of a walk with your loved one on the beach rather than seeing yourself happy at work! The important thing is to concentrate on feelings, rather than details. Think about how you will feel your positive intention in action – perhaps confident at work, calm at home or optimistic about a daily situation.

As you visualise, you may be caught up in unwanted thoughts or sensations, like: 'This is impossible', or: 'I see too many situations and can't focus on one'. If you are struggling, don't fight it. It is normal and part of your consciousness here and now. Just acknowledge the unwanted thought and then simply use the tension relax exercise on your entire body to let go through your out breath of the resistance you experience. Let it come and enjoy it. It is the positive resources of your consciousness that manifest and that will also help you deal with and create a better daily life.

It is encouraging to see how full of opportunity a whole day can be when you think of it slowly and carefully in this manner – we really feel the power of the present by creating it in the future. And we open ourselves to such potential once we have 'fixed' in our brain our ideas and hopes for the positive circumstances our future could hold.

Our Happy Next Day Visualisation

1. Start with a tratac and short Foundation Practice sitting.
2. Seated in the Pharaoh posture, use your intuition to guide you into finding a word that represents the state

you would like to feel in during your day. Let it come to you. Trust your consciousness to show you. Create the image of yourself living your day, starting in the morning then moving throughout your day, as if you were in your chosen positive state. Visualise what the day would look like, how you would wake up in the morning, what you would have for breakfast, what you would do during this day as you are able to stay connected with your positive state. How would it feel to be in that state as you observe your day? Maybe how you would dress, or what you would have for lunch; would you meet people, would you be at work, are you doing an activity that you like in this perfect, happy day? And how would you finish your day: what is for dinner, what happens after dinner? How would you spend your evening, or prepare for sleep?

3. Once you have ended your perfect day, sitting back in the relaxed posture, breathe deeply a few times to connect to the sensation you have stimulated through-out your day and send it into your 5 systems. Pause and inhale all the positives of the exercise, remembering how it felt within your body. Take the time you need to return to your usual level of vigilance, feel your feet on the floor and become fully present before opening your eyes. Now enjoy your phenodescription.

Doing this exercise in the sophroliminal state means that not only do you create this visualisation with will and control, but you will also be open to receiving information from the depths of your consciousness. This technique can be quite life-changing – it literally builds awareness of behaviours during the day and, through making adjustments from an inner perspective first, it leads to alterations in your outer reality. You might be surprised at what your consciousness brings to your great day, and what new insights are gained as to how you feel about your present day and the details that resonate with your true self.

As you repeat this exercise over time, you will be able to increasingly feel in your mind and body as your day goes out of balance. You will be able to see the triggers for this and can make the decision for change.

'I attended several sessions with Dominique during the late stages of my pregnancy, which helped me enormously with birth preparation physically, mentally and emotionally. Through the breathing exercises and gentle movements I was able to visualise a positive birth experience and overcome the fears of childbirth that were looming in the back of my mind. The techniques are simple and easy to use in everyday life, and with practice I am now able to identify tensions in my body, release them and calm myself into a totally relaxed state of being.' Kathy

Enjoy a Bright Future

Now we look further into the future. This exercise guides you to select a resource that will positively impact your future, such as to strengthen your confidence or your resilience, or to increase hope or relaxation. In doing so, it enables you to open yourself to new possibilities, to change your relationship with the future.

Often we're nervous of the future, worried about impending problems or uncertain about our life choices and how they might impact on us. Alternatively, some see the future only in a repetitive pattern as a continuation of our current life, without having the time and energy to think more radically or to choose bigger aims or dreams. It's easy to get into a rut and to see the only way forward as a continuation of how and where you are now. When we're bombarded with the stresses of life, it can be as if we are travelling in a tunnel, and we can only move forward towards the narrow view in front of us. It's impossible to see other options. These futurisations help us to open up possibilities, to embrace the potential and not just to view limitations. We are going to change our relationship with the future.

'With Sophrology, suddenly I had enthusiasm and energy and a vision for the future. I was looking for love, and I would do my practice in front of a picture of a couple who love each other – in front of a picture of Robert Redford and Barbra Streisand when they were young and in love. Every morning I would look at it and say, "This is what I want."' Penelope

Before you start, choose something in your future that you want to transform or something you want to go well.

You could have a specific goal, such as spending more time on a hobby or interest, or looking to make a change in your career path. It can be a small change or a general desire to find more joy in life or more freedom, or even to live a completely different life. Be very clear about your intention before you go into the exercise. As you visualise the change, it becomes real for the brain, and so the brain begins to prepare for this positive change. So it's working with intention, and it's working with the mind too, and as we also connect that experience with the body – through the key techniques initially – it's almost as if it's part of a conversation between the body and the mind, taking the confidence from the body to ground the change.

Again, feel no pressure to 'succeed' at this visualisation. Following the Foundation Practice, we are simply going to see ourselves in our new future – from about six months up to two years ahead. We are going to picture ourselves in a happy situation, with the intended transformation complete. Where will I be? What do I wear? What am I doing? Maybe I am on my own or with a partner that I now have in my life. Maybe I have found that job I am looking for or I am totally healed from my present situation. Just trust it to come to you in the sophroliminal state and, as with any Sophrology practice, if something uncomfortable or emotionally difficult arises, use your tension relax as many times as necessary. What is important is not what you do or do not manage to see, it is the simple effort of your brain following the positive intention that holds the magic.

Create Your Future Visualisation

1. Start with a tratac and short Foundation Practice.
2. From a fully relaxed state, sitting in the Pharaoh posture, let an image come to you, with yourself in it, of six months' time when you feel great. Now create your futurisation of the thing you want. Where are you? What time of the day is it? How are you dressed and how do you feel? Picture the scene and anyone else who is there at the time and fill it with detail – using all of your senses. Take the time to relax into the scene and to ensure that it is authentic to you.
3. At the end, pause and inhale all the positives of the exercise, remembering how the empowering experience felt within your body. Take the time you need to return to the presence of your body, feel your feet on the floor and become fully present before opening your eyes.
4. Write your phenodescription.

This is truly a Level 2 practice, projecting to creating the life you want. Doing this opens up the possibilities in your mind, and makes you more focused and creative in order to achieve your project. There is always a body component in the experience as we anchor our positive experience in our bodies with the breath.

What you will then create in your life doesn't need to be the exact replica of the situation, of course. We are training your inner resources in relation to your future, strengthening your ability to project yourself into a positive future.

Be Empowered by Your Past

Just as visualising our perfect day was a strong message to our consciousness about our potential for the future, taking a mental walk through a time in our past when we felt strong, confident, happy or positive brings this strength to our current and future life.

In order to enjoy our future, further strengthening our confidence is always a good idea. My clients are sometimes faced with feeling disarmed by a situation. They may lack confidence in relation to a specific event, like a talk they have to give at work or an important meeting or competition they would like to succeed in. I always start by telling them that confidence is already inside them, otherwise they wouldn't be sitting here. It takes confidence to go through life and even to ask for help and support. Even when they have been through adversity and dramatic situations, the simple fact they are sitting in front of me telling me about it tells me that they have plenty of incredible resources to move forward.

I use this simple Level 3 practice to support them to reconnect with their confidence. In the sophroliminal state, I invite them to find a positive memory, a moment when they felt empowered in succeeding at something. It's all too easy to remember times when we weren't happy with what we achieved, but often we don't take the time to recall the times when we were successful, and confident in our actions. You may be surprised at the positive things you can recall in the sophroliminal state. It doesn't need to be something huge, but something we felt good at accomplishing, or comfortable doing. By anchoring that positive experience in the body, you use this gift of confidence from the past to visualise yourself succeeding in the future.

The Empowering Past Visualisation

1. Begin sitting with the tratac and short Foundation Practice. Then, in the Pharaoh posture, look for a moment in your past when you felt fully confident and strong.
2. Try to recall all the details as you move through the event. Recall how you felt, and follow the response of your body as you recall your actions, conversations and the thoughts you had, where it is possible to remember.
3. Don't be afraid to push yourself to recapture how you truthfully felt at specific times of the day.
4. Finally, recall how you felt when you had achieved your aim – your confidence and how good it felt. Back in the sitting relaxed posture, finish with an exhale and a slow return.
5. For this practice, take the time to think through your phenodescription carefully and make some notes.

As you are now more practised in Sophrology, this is a wonderful practice to allow you to match the responses in your body to the actions of the past. Do they reflect your mood, and are there any surprises? I would expect you to be able to uncover some new truths about yourself through your sensations and responses.

Explore Your Life Purpose

This simple and important practice – inspired by Level 4 Sophrology – allows the mind–body connection to bring its deepest self-knowledge to you to aid you in choosing and bringing to your life a meaningful value as your guide. More than ever we can feel challenged or pressured by some of the values our society imposes on us. We might feel that we need to conform to what our family, community, media, school or company have transmitted or unconsciously pushed into our value system and beliefs.

You are going to engage your deep awareness and connection with the body, connecting with all the sensations of the body, and then 'ask' your body and mind to come up with a positive value. In this state of deep relaxation, your mind is at its full creative potential and you are able to tap into a deep personal wisdom regarding your reason for being. It can have very surprising results.

You will ask yourself what you value most in your daily life, or what you want to be or to achieve – all ways to tap into your key purposes. It's something positive, and it can be linked to your own individual self – maybe you want more freedom, love, respect – or it can be a value that you carry towards the group, like 'family' or a value of society. It could be freedom, warmth, respect for yourself and others, dignity, friendship, family, love, nature, humanity, community, society, eternity, divinity, universality, individuality, responsibility, or something completely different. Remember that there is no right or wrong choice.

It could be a sensation in your body, or maybe it's a value that motivates and steers you. Perhaps it is something you haven't fully considered before. Once your value has been made clear to you, you do a futurisation about how you want to live that way more fully. Choose a section of your life and visualise how you can immerse that value into that part of your daily life. In your mind, you bring that value awake or you are living that value in your daily life – perhaps you visualise ways of bringing nature into your family life, perhaps your thoughts centre around trust within a particular relationship or community through your career choices. By taking the time to explore your motivators and how they can become more significant in your daily life, you open the potential to bring huge fulfilment and opportunity to your future.

'Be Inspired, Be You' Visualisation

1. Once you have completed the Foundation Practice, tune into the body and mind from the Pharaoh posture to find a value that is true to your heart. Ask yourself, 'What is it that I value most in my daily life?' or, 'What would I like to value more?' Or just let the value come

to you. So it can be something that you've already explored or something entirely new that you would like to integrate into your life and see where it takes you.

2. Once you have your value chosen, then you view an aspect of your life through the lens of your choice, giving yourself the chance to visualise this value and how it shapes your life. What could it look like? How would it feel? Again, the power of the futurisation lies in the detail with which you build the experience. Use all your senses to create the future experience, demonstrating your value and how your life is different.

3. Sit back in the relaxed posture and finish with a few breaths to stimulate that value within you and do a slow return.

4. Enjoy your phenodescription.

You can perform this exercise with a different 'purpose' each time, and also remember to take the opportunity to let your body 'choose' your intention. In the higher levels of Sophrology, our purpose and values become more relevant (page 214) and we look to be guided by them and seek them out for a more meaningful life.

These four exercises are powerful motivators for the future. Some will find them easier than others, but be confident in your ability and remember to use the tension relax to help you if you struggle to stay focused within the visualisation. Enjoy and embrace what they tell you about yourself and your potential for the future.

How to Include Sophrology in Your Daily Life

The most important thing to remember is that including Sophrology in your everyday life should not be like adding another thing on your to-do list that is another stress! Please remember you are doing this for yourself so start where and when it is possible, even if it is very small steps to begin with. If you have really decided to start looking after yourself and to improve your life, your intention is set and things will start moving in the right direction.

Now that you have been through the many practices of this book, I hope that you have already found your own ways to adapt them. Think about what works well for you. Is it breathing that is most efficient in connecting and feeling present and full of energy? Maybe you particularly like one movement of Level 1 to help you ground and relax. Maybe one image or word really speaks to you to connect you with confidence or joy? All the vivance you have experienced are now stored in your positive library of resources, ready to be brought to awareness in your body and mind at any moment, so don't hesitate to use them. Here are some thoughts about how to make Sophrology even more powerful for you:

Remember that it is more efficient to do **short practices** every day than a long session every week. Repetition is the key.

1. Remember that there is **nothing to 'achieve'** in your path of self-discovery through Sophrology. Everything you experience is valid and is one step forward into greater awareness, presence and balance.

2. **Trust yourself and how you feel**. This is key – everybody is different in the way they experience the exercises, and therefore trusting what you feel is crucial. There will be exercises that work better than others for you, or that feel more natural. Always follow what makes you feel good. If something is uncomfortable, please adapt your position or simply leave it out for the moment, and come back to it later when you feel ready (or not!).

3. Think about your days, weeks and weekends: **when do you have time to plug in and include an exercise?** On your way to work, before you go home from work, before bed, after training perhaps? Use those times of day when you would just be checking emails or doing five minutes of jobs before or after something, to find time for Sophrology.

4. If you're still struggling to make time, remember that the time you spend practising Sophrology is **time that you will get back** through the results. Once you are more focused and have more energy, everything will flow more easily.

5. **The recordings are very useful at the beginning**, or if you need extra guidance or encouragement. Trust that you can close your eyes and find your way to tune in. It's a learning curve.

6. Trust that your practice and its benefits are **within you** after you have practised for a little while and that, on the go, at any time of your day, you are able to connect with what you have felt during the sessions and the **vital power of your consciousness**.

7. **Make Sophrology your own**: through the practice of the Sophrology principles and the supertools in this book, you will naturally develop your own ways to deal with situations and use the tools that work for you – whether it be The Reflex to cope with challenging situations, or The Bubble to defuse stressful days. When your mind takes over, reconnect with your body with a tool that you can remember on the go (The Pump, The Reflex Sign, The Body Halves) and do it on the spot.

8. Use the tension relax exercise during the day to **acknowledge and let go of your tension or difficult emotions** so they don't build up and then manifest physically or emotionally.

9. Remember to **set your intention** for your day, for a meeting, for a project, for your life, for your relationship – your practice will reinforce the positive energies.

10. Consciousness is infinite, so for those who are hungry for more, the method of Sophrology offers plenty more opportunities to carry on **your path of**

self-discovery to the next level of awareness, harmony and happiness.

11. **Share your Sophrology with others**, including kids and adolescents! You now know what works, and a simple observing the breath, a tension relax or a bubble can really make a difference to someone's day!

12. Remember that all your resources are inside you and that by connecting to the beauty surrounding you, to positive people, with activities you like, you will reinforce your happy feelings to become a **more confident and positive being**.

13. **Try to look at the world differently**, without judgement and staying open to something new every day – noticing more, reacting less and letting go. With this will come new meaning in every experience.

SOPHROFLASH!

If nothing else, taking a Sophroflash moment is a brilliant aid to connect regularly: to the good and the bad! Several times a day just take a moment to relax, tune into your systems and see what they say. Do a quick dive into your sophroliminal state and breathe. It will be beneficial in keeping your energy up and your stress levels down. Get used to the idea of your body being able to communicate vital information to you.

Finding Happiness with Sophrology

....

'Happiness cannot be travelled to, owned,
earned, worn or consumed. Happiness
is the spiritual experience of living every
minute with love, grace and gratitude.'
DENIS WAITLEY, MOTIVATIONAL
SPEAKER AND AUTHOR

....

Now that you have started your practice, you are surely starting to see the potential and transformation that a regular practice can bring. As we have seen, Sophrology offers tools to work with specific concerns as well as being a practice and a philosophy for life – from coping with the weight of daily stresses and tensions, to preparing for specific events and learning to be more present in our lives and bodies.

When we are regularly practising and accessing the sophroliminal state, there is a sense of greater clarity, openness and well-being that comes from within. Being able to live more and more in the present moment will mean that we are able to enjoy our lives even more. I really think that life is about enjoying the experiences we go through, even if there will be moments that are more difficult or require a different kind of presence. The happiness we are talking about is not something that is so far away that it cannot be reached, it is about living every moment with awareness and using our resources so we can confidently and happily be in the flow. When we are in tune with ourselves and have been able to create the conditions supporting our well-being, then happiness naturally emerges and is our foundation state, our energy and our norm.

That open and happy state only gets better as you progress through the 12 Levels of the method. The ultimate aim of the Sophrology practice is to access a state of harmony in consciousness called the 'sophronique state'. This is a state of consciousness where one is deeply connected to oneself and the world around, a state of clarity from which a person can exist with all their potential and authenticity, fully connected to life and the present moment. It is a state of inner harmony that we project to our existence.

These states are not meant to be just a part of your practice, with your eyes closed in the confined state of an office or your bedroom. As your practice deepens, the progressive change in the quality of your perceptions and experiences will change the way you live your daily life and how you go through its experiences. You will live Sophrology with open eyes, being able to use your potential and exist with a renewed sense of your personal values, embodied in your daily life.

'Finally when I was 50 I realised that now I needed to take that space for myself. To look into what makes me feel that way. It's not about being selfish to do that – it's essential.'
Maguelonne

Positivity Is Infectious

And it's not just about your own journey either. The gradual change you have started with the practice in this book will inevitably be noticed by the people you live or even work with. They might comment on your new zen attitude and be intrigued or even inspired by it! My dad decided to start Sophrology when he saw how it worked for me. Being a successful entrepreneur, he was dealing with a lot of pressures and was anxious at times. As Sophrology is a tailored approach, the path we each took with it was very different because we had different needs. I was able to discuss it with him, though, and to this day we still enthusiastically share our personal discoveries in Sophrology.

As my own Sophrologist Gill later taught me, and I now see it all the time in my practice, if one member of a family or group starts with Sophrology, other members of that family or group will sense it and may start some work on themselves, one way or another. Of course, we can't change people around us but we can start by ourselves and often things will start to shift. The vibe we carry around, our changes of attitude and behaviour, will be picked up – sometimes unconsciously. So working on yourself with

The Mind–Body Connection Check-in

At this point, you have practised Level 1 and experienced some of Level 2 of the Sophrology method, focusing on the body and mind and finding and strengthening their connection. Try one of the early exercises again now, such as the Tune into Your Body exercise (page 29) to notice the change in yourself. Compare your phenodescription now to the first time – how does it differ and, with your knowledge of Sophrology now, what do you feel differently in your body's response and your ability to notice it?

This is just the start of the deeper connection between your inner self and your body and mind, where the physical tensions you may manifest have meaning and where you are now freeing your body and mind from the tensions they absorb and creating a more positive present and future. Look at what has changed in the way you talk about your experience of your sensations and perceptions. Do you see an evolution, or themes that are coming back often? Your phenodescription is like taking a picture of your state and experience at one point in time in the practice. Try not to analyse it in depth, but rather observe with an open mind, as it gives you an interesting account of who you are and what is alive in your consciousness, what evolves, and what has worked for you.

Sophrology can be a very useful tool to break the cycle of negativity or tension you feel in a relationship.

A Taste of More Sophrology

Looking forwards, we can start to focus on new ways to your consciousness and deepen the connection. These aren't formal Sophrology exercises, but an invitation to bring something new to your journey into awareness.

In Levels 1 to 4, we are learning to tune into consciousness through body and mind, and leaving to the side for a moment all our preconceptions and beliefs, the background noise and all we have previously learnt so we can look at ourselves and the world through a new pair of eyes. We are learning to let go of our conditioning: 'It is necessary so our consciousness can live freely,' said Caycedo.

This stronger union of body and mind through the practice is what will allow consciousness to deploy its full power in the next cycle. Levels 5 to 8 form the Mastery Cycle of the method, a kind of conquest where we learn to tune into consciousness itself as a dynamic energy that is in us, which connects mind, body and soul and constantly evolves by nature. Using his observation and experiences of the greatest yogi, notably with sound and his phenomenological approach of consciousness, Caycedo's simple practices guide us on a path to realising further the connection between mind, body and soul through consciousness. Like the birth of the butterfly, Levels 9 to 12 form the Transformational Cycle. Not that we haven't transformed until now! It teaches how to stay in tune with our deepest self, going through our daily lives having discovered its value and learning to live and meet others in accordance with our deepest liberated self.

From the experience of a few moments of harmony at the beginning of the practice of Sophrology, we are now able to stay in this happy state – the sophronique state – much longer and while away from the practice, grounded in ourselves and able to respond to events in accordance with what we are. Think about playing the piano; it takes time and practice to be able to play a full melody or even a concerto! As with everything, if you find a little time for regular practice you get more out of it. But these practices remain simple to do even if their intentions are deep. That's the beauty of Sophrology!

Contemplation: 'The quiet and liberated mind'

As part of Level 2 and beyond, Sophrology encompasses the practice of 'contemplation', which Caycedo based on the Buddhist practice. In Buddhism, meditation is known as 'bhavana', which in translation means 'cultivating' or 'growing'. This practice combines training the possibilities of the mind to be creative, calm and focused and expand beyond the limits of the body with the development and increased knowledge of the self.

You tune into the systems but with a different intention and perspective. Instead of looking for sensations, you take a refined observation of them, their space and shape, training a more perceptive observation of the system as if from outside yourself before you release the tension.

Training our ability to contemplate is very useful in our daily life. It will help us take a step back in everyday situations to think before we react, and to be more creative in the way we respond to events. It will support the mind to further open itself to new possibilities of seeing, thinking, hearing, sensing and even tasting differently, changing our perceptions. It further supports the unveiling of consciousness and helping us to unlock our potentials.

Contemplation Exercise

Try the object visualisation used at the end of Level 1 (see page 122) to experience the relaxing and enlightening experience of contemplation to focus the mind. This time, though, take your observation and use it on your own body, viewing yourself as if from the outside – sitting or standing – and noting your shape, form and dress. Using your body rather than a general household object requires a greater level of non-judgement and clarity.

It requires quite a strength of focus to take a greater step back from your own mind, situations and emotions. You are looking at things from unfamiliar angles – differently and without judgement – and training your mind to be more free and mobile, and to view the world around you both more objectively and as something less fixed in its current state.

Nature – a walking meditation

Caycedo didn't explore the opportunities of the natural world when devising his practice, but being immersed in nature is one of the easiest ways of becoming more relaxed and grounded – with our own selves and the world around us. And we don't need to embark on a month-long expedition into the wilderness to feel the effects (there has been a wonderful study in Toronto by neuroscientist Professor Marc Berman[*] about the effects on health of living on an urban street with trees compared to living on a street without). Just finding a few minutes each day to spend in the garden and listen to birdsong or a detour through a green space in your lunch break will help you feel more calm and energised. There are numerous studies into the effects of nature on our brains – influencing our ability to focus and concentrate, to reason more clearly and in the reduction of negative thinking. There is also research looking at the significant changes to cortisol (the hormone linked to chronic stress and the resulting side-effects) when being in the natural world is part of our daily life. It feels as if we are just at the beginning of rediscovering how important being in nature is to restore and harmonise our bodies and minds in powerful ways.

[*] Berman, Marc G. et al., Neighborhood greenspace and health in a large urban center. *Scientific Reports* 5, Article number: 11610, 2015

Nature Exercise

Try finding a time to walk in nature as a regular part of your life, and link it with your Sophrology practice. See this time as time for yourself – nurturing time – rather than being tempted to turn it into a mad dash to run some errands or just a means to get somewhere else. Start with a simple body scan at home or outdoors, in order to ground yourself, then walk with awareness and freedom. Use this time to look around you and try to look at things with new eyes, as if for the first time.

Start by walking consciously – feel the weight of your body and your feet meeting the ground. Be aware of how your joints are moving and what your body is doing to propel you forward. Then listen to your breathing and make sure you are breathing through your abdomen. Use the time to release your tensions and breathe in more energy. If you feel tense in any system of the body, breathe it out as you walk.

After a while, take a moment to sit and note your surroundings and immerse yourself in your present. Look at the nature around you and work through your senses (part of Level 5 in Sophrology) to widen your experience and to awaken your body. If you wish, choose a word or focus for your walk – invite 'love' or 'compassion' or something that you wish to cultivate in your daily life by taking a moment to connect with this positive energy with the breath.

Sound - Tuning In

About the use of sound in Sophrology, Caycedo said: 'The use of sound profoundly attracted my attention since my time in the Himalayas. Sounds as a body percussion: I had never seen this. As a neurologist, I couldn't not look into it. This great yogi was fascinating . . . he literally vibrated with music ... vibrations of the yogi were physically felt; he could direct them endlessly with his own wish towards different part of his body. He was only like a big tuning fork and the vibrations were more or less deep depending on the place he was directing them; the ones in his arm were different than the one in his vertebral column, or the base of his neck, or in his throat. It was simply amazing.'

Sound and music as a form of therapy or mood enhancer is something I have studied in depth. We can all feel the effect of our favourite song when we're out jogging or stuck in traffic to lift our mood and our performance. Neurological studies show that the rhythm of sound that we experience changes our brainwaves and our breathing patterns. As part of Level 5 in Sophrology, we use sound and humming as a transformative tool in our systems, and we learn how to listen to our bodies with sound. Using the power of sound – mostly through our voice – we are 'percussing' our bodies, our cells. Using audible and non-audible sounds, grounded in our bodies and with a clear intent, we connect with our cells' energy and their potential through sound, as a vibration we notice in the body.

In Sophrology, we often use different sounds for each system. Often people 'feel' certain sounds better than others, or maybe you feel comfortable using the universal 'Om'. I find that humming is a particularly effective way to elongate the out breath for a calming effect, and something I often use with my clients. I call it a 'sonic cuddle'!

Sound Exercise

Try a simple humming exercise:

Do a quick Foundation Practice, then choose a space within you that needs healing – maybe you have a headache, a sore shoulder or some digestive issues – or a system is particularly tense. Start humming, and put your hand on your tummy and feel the vibration there. Experiment with the pitch and volume until it feels comfortable. Now, think of the system you are going to work on and to which you want to send your healing and sound energy. Place your hand on the corresponding integration point for the system, and feel the vibrations pushing energy into that system, bringing healing and calm. Try to feel the effects of the sound in the body.

This could be a simple 5 or 10-minute practice, a balancing practice that supports a recovery or body awareness.

If you are drawn to carry on this fantastic journey into consciousness with Sophrology and discover what the next levels have in store, it is useful to find the help of a practitioner or to join a Sophrology group (see page 217 for more information). Having a community of like-minded individuals with whom you can share your phenodescription and learn from each other's experience is very enriching (as I have found as a student and a teacher).

CASE STUDY: **CATHERINE**
– 'IT'S ABOUT TUNING IN
TO WHAT YOU NEED.'

Catherine, 39, is an artist. She was diagnosed with severe ME when she was 12 and was hospitalised on and off. By her early twenties, a combination of various therapies had brought her ME to a less extreme level, after which she was diagnosed with Post Traumatic Stress Disorder from the trauma of living with her health issues. She was struggling with her energy levels and severe stress when she started Sophrology.

'I had ME very badly as a teenager and it was an extremely stressful and traumatic time as people didn't really understand, and I had difficulties with the doctors. In my early twenties, through a combination of medication, nutrition and therapies, I started to improve, and from my late twenties, I was able to work a little. Once I was much better, things just hit me and then I was formally diagnosed with Post

Traumatic Stress Disorder. I just felt numb emotionally – I hadn't dealt with any of the stuff that had happened. Now I see a psychotherapist and Dominique.

With stress, you cut off and disconnect. You end up in your head a lot, which is what happened to me. My understanding of stress is that it's not just your mind, it's your body too. There is a physiological approach – the 'fight or flight' response – and as much as doing something like meditation helps, it's really difficult with your heart pounding in flight mode. But in Sophrology it's about the body too, you're doing things.

I think also about how disconnected I was, and the body awareness of Sophrology, which has been helpful in terms of PTSD and in a physical way as well, connecting me with body in a way that I'd forgotten how to be with my illness. I had cut off from myself. From an early age, the doctors and others trying to help me had said 'eat this' and 'do that'. If you don't have any physical awareness, you're just on autopilot and you don't really think. It's about tuning into what you need. And I think that's relevant to any illness, particularly any chronic illness. The whole premise of modern conventional medicine is that you get told what to do by a doctor. Now I know that I need to listen to myself, use my intuition and awareness. I can see Sophrology is part of that – learning to trust yourself.

The Sophrology exercises really helped me. Exercises take you somewhere – a sense of progression. Awareness helps you focus on different things, on your body and your consciousness. That's been helpful too. And then I feel spacey a lot. So the grounding exercises are good – in a physical way.

That's the main thing – it's a whole-body thing. It's a 360-degree approach. If you have something quite complex/long-term then, yes, diet and psychotherapy can help but you need to include everything. For chronic illnesses, some people don't get that something that helps you sleep better makes a huge difference to your everyday life. Or something that gives you a sense of well-being.

And working in a group is good for me too. You can react differently in a group. I realised I feel a bit numb. You learn something from the community – all trying to get better, balance their lives. Everyone's different. I find in yoga that people are competitive – what you can do, what you wear. In Sophrology, you have to be true to yourself. You see that to some it some-times comes naturally, sometimes harder. It helps me remember we're not aiming for perfection – just the journey.'

How to Be Sophro

To 'Be Sophro' is what I call being in a state of balance and harmony. It is about being content and happy in our daily lives. It is a dynamic state that goes hand-in-hand with our capacity to positively align our body and mind with the world around us. It is to be aware of the infinite potential of learning, discovery and healing through life.

It brings us more deeply connected to life and gives us the headspace, energy and capacity to want to make the most of it for ourselves and for others around us. This positive state is contagious and you will soon recognise those who are on the same journey in one way or another. And having learnt to have more self-acceptance and compassion for yourself through your process will certainly make you a better friend, parent, partner and family member.

Don't stay alone, share the good and the bad, and don't be afraid of being authentic. The world wants to know about who you are, what you think and feel, and to see your individual talents and capacities emerge. I deeply believe that we all contribute to this world, some very loudly and in the eyes of others, and some more quietly and with subtlety. For those who are doers and have great plans, Sophrology will be like a great friend to support your actions, increasing your confidence, freeing your work capacity and keeping you in balance along the way. For those who are on a more contemplative journey or already greatly experienced in the field of self-discovery, Sophrology can help you widen and further enhance your experience. For those who are both, you will use Sophrology at different times, in different ways.

Sophrology hasn't solved everything in my life. I'm still an active working mum – worrying about my family and making decisions about the hours that I work to try to maintain balance and keep inspired. Sophrology has given me tools that I can rely on in daily life – ways to be sure that I can be true to myself and enjoy my life. We need to find those 10 minutes each day. Just switch on the recording before you go to bed, or when you have a toilet break or are outside in nature. Start with what is possible. And from the moment you close your eyes, you are beginning to make that connection, you're starting to deal with things in a different way. You will find more space, you will value things differently, you will give yourself permission to make changes to your life.

Remember that in the middle of dealing with everything and juggling life, you are the centre. And if that centre is not happy, nothing around it can work. So those 10 minutes that can be so difficult to find are key – they are crucial to maintaining the balance for the steps ahead.

It's too easy to live our life at maximum pace – juggling, running around and saying yes to everything. But we forget that we're not running a sprint here – life is a marathon and we should make sure it feels meaningful so we can enjoy it. And once you've managed to slow down a little and connect, you can become creative about your life. You will have clarity. You will have greater focus. You will become an observer of your life and know that you can change it. There's nothing stopping you from changing what you want to change. Use Sophrology to find more freedom and inspiration in daily life. And in doing so, find yourself and your place in the world. It's all a journey – so trust in yourself, and spread the love!

Please feel free to join me and my BeSophro community to practice more Sophrology, share your questions, experience or phenodescriptions. I would love to hear from you! My website is www.be-sophro.com.

Q AND A

Your Sophrology questions answered

What will be my experience with a Sophrologist?

Your Sophrologist will guide you with his or her voice through the different parts of a tailored practice – they listen and guide without judgement or analysis. A Sophrologist may be specialised in one or several areas – stress management, self-development, corporate, children, sport, birth preparation or sleep. They usually mention it on their website but it is always worth asking too. Sophrology is often a tool that someone has acquired on top of other knowledge and experiences. It is not unusual to find a Sophrologist who has a background as a midwife, osteopath, doctor, education specialist, psychologist, or someone who has worked in the business or corporate world.

Session after session, what we call the 'alliance' between the client and the Sophrologist will naturally develop. The 'alliance' defines the type of relationship, and stresses that the Sophrologist is a guide and support, not strictly a teacher (it is not the type of relationship where the therapist is superior in some way). Ideally, your connection will feel authentic and based on trust, thanks to the empathic and supportive space created by the Sophrologist (who needs to be aware of and responsible for his or her own state of being, words and actions). The client is guided by the Sophrologist in the learning of the Sophrology method and supported by the meaningful exchanges they have. These exchanges will be used by the Sophrologist to create his or her 'terpnos logos', the specific language used by the Sophrologist to support the vivance of the client during the practice.

Once you have mastered the practical aspects of the Sophrology practice by repeating it sufficiently, you won't need the Sophrologist's voice to be guided into the sophroliminal state or to activate your vivance. You will connect very easily and master this practice. But I also advise regular guidance from a Sophrologist, as it often allows you to go a step further and deeper and is enjoyable and more relaxing because of the phenomenological encounter that happens within the alliance.

What is a Caycedian Sophrologist?

A Caycedian Sophrologist is someone who has trained in a Caycedian School (there are more than 50 across Europe) and therefore has been trained using the 12 Levels of Caycedian Sophrology, the method created by Alfonso Caycedo. They are other types of curriculum available to learn Sophrology – some remain very close to Caycedo's approach and others have extracted part of the method to serve specific therapeutic or coaching purposes.

Here are the 12 Levels of the Sophrology Method.

		Main Focus	Inspiration	Exploration
Cycle 1	Level 1	Body as an Anchor	Yoga	Inhabit your Present
	Level 2	Mind and its Infinite Possibilities	Meditation	Trust your Future
	Level 3	Union of Body and Mind	Zen	Empowered by your Past
	Level 4	My Values as my Guide	Existential Phenomenology	Living the Present Moment
Cycle 2	Level 5	Consciousness is Energy	Sound Yoga (Nada) – Sounds of Voice	Sound to Activate Consciousness
	Level 6	Consciousness as a Universal Energy	Use of Inaudible Sounds	Finding Harmony in Consciousness
	Level 7	Consciousness and its Origins	Sound Yoga (Nada) – Sounds of Voice	Tuning into my Cellular Memory
	Level 8	Consciousness as a Creative Energy	Sound Yoga (Nada) – Sounds of Voice	Tuning into my Foetal Life
Cycle 3	Level 9	Feeling Free in My Daily Life	Phenomenology	Tuning into My Freedom to Be
	Level 10	Rediscovering the Objects Around Me	Phenomenology	The Value of Objects Around Me
	Level 11	Rediscovering People Around Me	Phenomenology	The Value of People Around Me
	Level 12	Living my True Self	Phenomenology	Tuning into Freedom, Responsibility and Dignity

What is the 'terpnos logos'?

The way in which the Sophrologist addresses their client to guide them in the practice and the wording they use is called the 'terpnos logos' in Sophrology. This term chosen by Caycedo was originally used by Plato to describe a type of healing word aiming at the soul, and creating a state of calm, harmony and awareness for body and mind.

The tone of voice should be harmonious and warm, and the rhythm relatively slow, to inspire a state of relaxation and ease. They give practical information to the client about the moves, the posture and the breathing, but most importantly, the sound must engender trust and receptivity so the client can fully connect with their sensations and perception and make the most of their experience. The vocabulary is specific, for example in the way we go through the body scan or support people in their creative visualisation. It also needs to be adapted to the age, background and aims of the person we have in front of us.

This is crucially different from the suggestion language that can be used in hypnosis, although, as in Sophrology, the client remains fully in control and consciously present. At all times, his or her freedom in the process should be encouraged, in order to discover what works for them and to slowly become more and more independent with their practice.

The terpnos logos follows certain rules, to be efficient, but each Sophrologist also brings their own mark to it. It is informed by their own learning, experience of the practice and their connection to themselves and their consciousness, and to a certain extent by personality, of course. It becomes a creative space for the Sophrologist, guided by their intuition of the client's needs, abilities and goals.

This way of communication with our clients is a skill the Sophrologist needs to master and I also believe that this way of communication is a deeply comforting and healing tool, and that through the vibration of the Sophrologist's voice there is something less tangible that connects both consciousnesses and is deeply transformative for both parties.

Like with any human exchange, especially a therapeutic one, you will find some terpnos logos that resonate less or more with you. Some you will immediately trust and benefit from, some you will find more difficult to guide you into your own experience. Don't be afraid to work with several Sophrologists to find out which alliance will support you best.

The voice of my own dear Sophrologist Gill still resonates in my head when I tune in, and having done so many years of Sophrology guided by her word and energy has certainly left an imprint on mine. I also remember very vividly the voice of world-renowned Sophrologist Raymond Abrezol, which instantly instilled a sense of self-confidence in my practice and supported the discoveries of my inner resources very strongly. As I was guided by him in the practice I always felt that everything was possible if I just deeply connected. Each Sophrologist I have encountered has something deep to transmit and no one does it in exactly the same way. That's the beauty of it all.

Should I do Sophrology in a group?

Yes! All Sophrology experience is valuable for assorted reasons. In a group, you have the chance to experience it differently, and to gain from a more collaborative effort. I find groups bring diverse energies to the practice, and their communication before and after the practice obviously feels supportive and illuminating to each other. Many of my long-term clients continue to attend group classes regularly in order to build a different relationship within Sophrology.

How long does it take to become a qualified Sophrologist?

As I have said earlier, there are a variety of curricula, which have various lengths. The Caycedian training I did in Switzerland and then in Andorra with Dr Alfonso Caycedo was over four years and took 500 hours to complete. The reason why Sophrology is usually taught over a few years is to allow the practitioner to develop his or her own experience of the practice, its benefits and deep transformation. This is key to being able to guide your client through their journey of self-discovery.

Are there any contraindications to Sophrology?

As I'm keen to emphasise, Sophrology is appropriate for all levels of fitness and mobility as long as the person is fully conscious and has normal faculty. All of the exercises can be adapted to suit and nothing should be difficult to achieve or leave you in discomfort. If you have any doubt or are under medical treatment, always ask your doctor first.

What if I can't stay focused?

This is very common feedback! Firstly, for those who have tried meditation and mindfulness and have this problem, I do find that Sophrology suits you much better due to its movement and actions. It naturally works towards stilling the brain and bringing focus. But even if you do find it difficult, I suggest that you acknowledge it and carry on your practice, keeping to very short practices to start with and slowly increasing the time you spend with your eyes closed. If you need to, do a quick tension relax before you carry on. If you need to try again at a better time, do that without judgement. If you are still struggling, ask for advice from a qualified Sophrologist, who will be able to tailor the method to your very specific needs.

Can you tell us a little about your specialities?

I feel very privileged to be able to work with a wide variety of people. I think each story is unique and my role is to support the person or group in finding what they are looking for. To witness the moment where the individual connects with their own resource and understands how they can move forward is a gift. Giving people tools and strategies for stress management and self-development is key in this age and should be widely available, as it can completely change the dynamic in people's life and contributes to positive change in society. My other speciality is around birth preparation and parenthood. Sophrology is a fantastic way to prepare for birth, promoting natural birth as well as supporting women through other journeys. Sophrology goes beyond preparing for the big day. From dealing with IVF or discomforts during pregnancy, to body image and supporting the huge changes pregnancy brings in term of body, mind and daily life, to preparing both parents for the arrival of the baby and to start bonding, to breastfeeding, lack of sleep or any other challenge a parent can face, Sophrology supports parents in finding more balance, confidence and happiness as well as feeling in tune with their deepest values.

Can children practise Sophrology?

Yes of course! And they can start as early as in the womb, bene-fitting from their mother's practice. Mothers who have done Sophrology during their pregnancy will often create a very strong and confident bond with their child, which will support its development. Working with young children requires a specific approach and training in Sophrology, using the princi-ples of phenomenology and body awareness and making them more accessible through play, stories and having fun. Sophrologie Ludique, created in 1985 by Claudia Sanchez and Ricardo Lopez, former students of Caycedo, is a branch of Sophrology that has developed tools to work with children and adolescents. Through structured and spontaneous play, the child learns to get in touch with his or her deeper self and inner resources. This simple way to accessing Sophrology has also become part of the general knowledge and adaptation of Sophrology for adults (as we are all children at heart!).

What other lifestyle advice do you give your clients alongside the practice of Sophrology?

The way I work with my clients in individual sessions is highly tailored. I use my experience as a former osteopath, as well as everything I have learnt along the way, to support them further if necessary. During our initial conversations I often hear a lot of information about their health and worries and that's very useful to complement Sophrology with other helpful solutions. As they become calmer and have more energy through the practice, they will naturally start to reflect more on what they eat or what they could do to maintain and further increase their well-being. In some cases, especially with chronic issues, a multi-disciplinary approach will be the winning solution. Whether it is nutrition, exercise, bodywork or homeopathy, everything else the client does will be supported by the awareness they have created with Sophrology.

Where can I download the audio guided exercises?

They are downloadable from my website: www.be-sophro.com/the-life-changing-power-of-sophology.

ACKNOWLEDGEMENTS

My deepest thanks and gratitude:

To Frédéric, my precious husband without whom none of this would have been possible and who makes our lives so special.

To Mylene P, for your constant presence and loving care.

To my clients for their trust and the journeys we share. Special thanks to those who have participated in this book.

To all my teachers – and specifically to Gill Thévoz – for your support, guidance and passion. To Alfonso Caycedo for his beautiful creation.

To Natalia Caycedo for our precious exchange.

Many thanks to Claudia Sanchez and Ricardo Lopez for making an exception and allowing me to reproduce their own specific SDN Point Exercise in my Foundation Practice 'On the Go'.

To Brigitte R, Alexandra B, Paola B and Kate S for your time and precious inputs.

To all the people and colleagues who have helped me build and support BeSophro. A special thanks to Paola B, Reena P, Lorinda P, Kate and Duncan S and Kate L.

To my parents, my sister and her family, and Frédéric's family; to my special friend Valérie P for her incredible support and to everybody in my tribe here in the UK and abroad for your love.

To Liz Gough and her wisdom for finding me and supporting this book.

To Kate Latham, for the quality of your support and the friendship we have developed.

To Amanda Preston, for kindly and efficiently introducing me into the book world.

To Juliet Percival for the beautiful drawings. To the whole team at Yellow Kite, notably Holly Whitaker, Veronique Norton, Caitriona Horne and Melis Dagoglu to name a few. Your great work, kindness and motivation was amazing, and thank you to everybody else who has helped us spread the message about this book.

To life and love, for being able to live each day and share this life with my son and all of you.

Where is Sophrology From?

1 This started after statistics drawn up in 1994, 1995 and 1996 by *Groupe Mutuel* – one of the largest health insurance firms in Switzerland – showed that clients of the Association of Sophroprophylaxia [i.e. people regularly practising Sophrology] cost the insurance company approximately 30 per cent less than the average insured person.

INDEX